92
JONES

Atkinson, Linda

Mother Jones: the
most dangerous
woman in America

DATE			
OCT 25 '79			
MR 09 '90			
Biundo			
DE 05			

MotherJones

Mother Jones

THE MOST DANGEROUS WOMAN IN AMERICA

BY LINDA ATKINSON

CROWN PUBLISHERS, INC.
New York

I would like to thank my editor, Donna Brooks, for her suggestions, her questions, and the encouragement she gave me all along the way; Earl Dotter, photo-journalist for the UMW *Journal*, for his interest and help in finding and obtaining photographs; J. C. Ricker, Dean of the Faculty of Education, University of Toronto; and Nancy Young, Reference Librarian, for their kind assistance.

Most of all, I would like to thank my husband, Bill, and my son, Willie. They always make everything worthwhile.

PHOTO CREDITS: Brown Brothers, 85; Chicago Historical Society, II, 41, 42, 47, 54, 68, 74, 75, 235; Coles Publishing Company Limited, Ontario, Canada, 18–19; Library of Congress, 116–117, 119, 157; Memphis/Shelby County Public Library, 26, 31, 35; New York Public Library, Picture Collection, 11, 88, 121, 146, 160; United Electrical Radio and Machine Workers of America, 62–63, 125; United Mine Workers of America, 6, 82–83, 96–97, 101, 106–107, 137, 140–141, 172, 179, 189, 190, 197, 200–201, 206, 209, 233; United Steelworkers of America, 215, 221, 224.

10   9   8   7   6   5   4   3   2   1

The text of this book is set in 12 pt. Caslon.
The illustrations are black-and-white photographs reproduced in halftone.

Library of Congress Cataloging in Publication Data
Atkinson, Linda.   Mother Jones, the most dangerous woman in America.
Bibliography: p.   Includes index. Summary: Traces the life and career of an Irish-born labor leader whose work began in the 1870's before the advent of strong unions and labor laws and continued for more than fifty years. 1. Jones, Mary Harris, 1830-1930. 2. Women in trade-unions—United States—Biography. [1. Jones, Mary Harris, 1830-1930. 2. Labor unions—Biography] I. Title. HD8073.J6A74 1978   331.88′092′4 [B] [92]
ISBN 0-517-53201-8   77-15863

For my mother, Sara,
with love.

✿ CONTENTS ✿

MotherJones

✖ INTRODUCTION ✖

*All the world's history has produced no more savage
and brutal times than these, and this nation will
perish if we do not change these conditions.*

MOTHER JONES, 1919

She was a handsome woman with calm blue eyes and a firm,
friendly handshake. A reporter described her as warm and
straightforward and said she was "probably the most patriotic
citizen this country has ever known." But a prosecuting attorney
in West Virginia pointed to her in a courtroom and said: "There
sits the most dangerous woman in America." Both the reporter
and the prosecutor were right.

Mary Jones was a labor leader. She was a spectacular,
controversial woman in an occupation—and a time—filled with
danger. Beginning in the 1870s and continuing for over fifty
years, Mary went to coal mines, train yards, factories, and logging
camps to meet with workers and help them struggle against
conditions that amounted, she said, to slavery. In those days that
kind of work was called "agitating." Today we might call it
"consciousness-raising." Mary called it "hell-raising."

1

"My life's work," she said, "has been to educate the worker to a sense of the wrongs he has had to suffer, and does suffer—and to stir up the oppressed to a point of getting off their knees and demanding that which I believe to be rightfully theirs."

America was just becoming an industrial nation when Mary started out. Steelyards and trains, factories and cities, were new. There were no strong unions then, and no laws to protect the rights of working people. The man who owned a business determined the number of hours his employees would work and decided what their wages would be. The majority of working people put in twelve and fourteen hours a day for wages that were pitifully low. They were not consulted or given any voice in the way their work was to be done.

"We are the rich," one businessman said. "We own America. We got it, God knows how, but we intend to keep it."

Mary was determined not to let them.

She was not intimidated by wealth or power, and called some of America's mightiest millionaires "pirates" and "high-class burglars." She once urged John D. Rockefeller, Jr. to visit the mines he owned in Colorado. If he did, she said, and helped the workers there, he would become "one of the greatest of Americans." Rockefeller said, "I am afraid you are inclined to throw compliments." "Oh, no," Mary replied. "I am much more inclined to throw bricks."

She was not afraid to criticize the government or to accuse public officials of selling out to millionaires and protecting the interests of crooks. To a man imprisoned in West Virginia for stealing a pair of shoes, she said, "What a shame. If you had stolen a railroad they would have made you a Senator."

The press often accused Mary of inciting the people to

violence. And sometimes she did. "You ought to be out raising hell!" she said to a group of strikers' wives in New York. "This is the fighting age! Put on your fighting clothes! America was not discovered by Columbus for the bunch of blood-sucking leeches who are now living off us!"

At another, calmer time, Mary explained that she did not believe in violence, but she did believe that "when force is used to hinder the worker in his attempt to gain that which is his, he has the right to fight force with force."

Most of the time, however, Mary could claim that the highest laws in the land, the laws of the Constitution of the United States, were on her side. The employers denied their workers' right to freedom of speech. They denied them freedom of assembly. Their gunmen denied them the right to liberty—and life. And the conditions under which men and women were forced to work denied them the right to the pursuit of happiness. With spirit, intelligence, and a powerful sense of compassion, Mary helped them to struggle for the freedom and dignity which, she said, was every American's birthright. That is why the reporter called her a patriot, and why other people considered her so dangerous.

Mary worked until she was well over ninety years old. She had no money. Her only possessions were the clothes she was wearing. Yet she crossed and recrossed the nation, going wherever she could be of help. She lived, as she put it, "wherever there is a fight." She stood up for the working poor when no one else would. She talked to them. She spoke for them. She fought alongside them. She was arrested, jailed, threatened at gunpoint. But she remained in the struggle. "I am not afraid," she said on one occasion. "I am not afraid of the pen, or the scaffold, or the sword. I will tell the truth wherever I please."

❧ ONE ❧

IRELAND

On a sunny day in May, in the year 1930, Mother Jones celebrated her one-hundredth birthday. In Chicago, New York, Denver, Seattle, and dozens of other cities throughout the United States, people gathered in her honor. Hundreds of friends and admirers came to the farmhouse in Maryland where she was living. The flowers and gifts they brought covered the lawn.

Mother Jones was living with Mr. and Mrs. Walter Burgess, a retired coal miner and his wife. They had invited her to stay with them a year earlier, when rheumatism and, as one doctor put it, pure exhaustion, had begun to confine her more and more often to bed. Still, she never "retired." She had fought for the rights of working people for over fifty years, and even when her great age made it impossible for her to leave her home, she remained deeply involved. She always had a warm smile for the friends and workers who came to see her. She read newspapers and journals, gave her views to the press and her encouragement to the people. She could not go out and join them, but she longed to. "I'm just an old warhorse," she said to a reporter, "ready to go into battle but too worn out to move."

During her last months she called John Walker, an old friend, to her bedside. He had given her $1,000 several years earlier, when she was in the hospital and needed the money badly. Now he was trying to build a new union, and Mother Jones returned the money to him. "I know of no better use for it," she said, wishing only that she could live long enough to see him succeed in his efforts.

"If I could get about on my legs," she told a reporter on her ninety-ninth birthday, "I would be out in the field organizing workers instead of idling away my time in bed."

Now, on her one-hundredth birthday, her blue eyes sparkled in her frail, thin face, and her smile was bright as she was helped to the table under the apple trees. There she was presented with a cake topped with a hundred candles. She laughed as her friends pinned a corsage of sweetpeas on her—first protesting, "Hell! I've never worn these things in my life!"

Paramount News was there to film her, and Mother Jones, who had only seen a "talkie" once in her life, was delighted. Her voice was clear and strong and she looked directly into the camera as she told America's working people to "stick together and be loyal to one another."

When the filming was over, the cake was served and the party broke up into small groups of people. They chatted under the warm Maryland sun and gathered to listen to Mother Jones talk about some of the things she had seen and done in a lifetime that spanned a century. She had grown up before the Civil War and

Mother Jones at her one-hundredth birthday party, May 1, 1930.

had attended speeches given by Abraham Lincoln. She had driven in horse-drawn buggies and watched the first automobiles—"delightful contraptions" she called them—slowly take over the roads. She had seen electric lights come into use, and railroads reach across the continent to the Pacific Ocean. She had seen cities grow where villages had been, and factories replace fields and farms. And she had seen landowners and factory owners become rich and powerful, while wage-earners—their employees—lived in poverty. She had thrown her talents and energy into their struggle to be treated decently. Over the years, she had had many close calls, as businessmen, armed guards, even government soldiers tried to stop her. She had faced them all and on her hundredth birthday proudly remembered how "one old woman, with her head gray, had scared hell out of the whole bunch."

"If they want to hang me, let them hang me," she said once. "But when I am on the scaffold, I'll cry 'Freedom for the working class!' "

Where did this amazing woman come from? How did she become a leader of coal miners, textile workers, steelworkers, thousands of people from every corner of the United States? The story of Mother Jones begins in Ireland, in the green and rolling hills of County Cork. There she was born, Mary Harris, in the year 1830. (Historians cannot be certain that that date is correct—some records suggest she was born later. But it is the date Mary herself always gave, and most people accept it.) Her family was a peasant family. They had lived on the land for as long as anyone could remember.

County Cork, like much of Ireland, is lovely to look at. Wild swans wander at the shores of its clear blue lakes. Heather covers the hillsides in the spring. But in the 1800s, the people there, as in most of Ireland, were desperately poor. By the time Mary was born, Ireland was the scene of savage fighting between the peasants and the "gentry," the upper-class people, most of them British, who owned almost all the farmland. "I was born in revolution," Mary used to say. And so she was.

Mary, the firstborn child of Richard and Mary Harris, lived with her parents and two brothers in a one-room thatched cottage made of straw and mud. It had no running water and no windows, and because it was built low against a hillside for support, the dampness of the earth was ever present. Even with a fire going in the fireplace, the cottage was never really warm or dry.

Similar cottages were home to thousands of peasants throughout Ireland. The cold, the bad air, and the dirt made them breeding grounds for disease. Illness was common, and almost every illness became an epidemic. Doctors could do little more than advise the peasants to "fill up the holes in the floor," "wash out the hut with soap and water and lime," and "get fresh air even if you must break through the walls to do so."

Mary's parents did not own their cottage or the small plot of land beside it. Like most of their neighbors, they were tenants— "cottager tenants," or "cotters" for short. For the use of the cottage and land, they paid a monthly rent to a landlord. To earn money, they worked as hired hands on his estate. They could not earn very much money, because work was not always available— and even when it was, wages were very low. For food, they depended entirely on what they could raise themselves. Like most cotters, Mary and her family lived on potatoes and oatmeal and an occasional herring. When they could afford to keep a cow, they had milk as well. Meat was only for the gentry.

Though life on a cotter holding was hard, the "revolution" Mary remembered might not have happened had it not been for a sharp rise in the number of evictions during the 1820s. In those years, landlords were trying to get higher incomes from their land. Some raised the rents. Cotters who could not pay were forced to leave. Other landlords cleared their land entirely—evicting all tenants—and turned it into pastureland. "We discover," said one landlord, "that grazing cows are more profitable than cottager tenants." Mary's parents managed to keep up with the rent on their holding and were not evicted. But in the 1820s, hundreds of cotters in County Cork—and hundreds of thousands throughout Ireland—were. Without shelter, even the crude shelter of a thatched cottage, and without land on which to raise even potatoes, an evicted peasant was helpless. He had to beg for food, or steal it, or starve. There were no organized charities or government agencies to help him.

By the year of Mary's birth, evicted peasants could be seen on every road and byway in Ireland, sick, undernourished, and ragged, begging for food and shelter. One traveler said that the "cries of the hungry fill the air," and that he could "feel the countryside seething." Soon, he declared, "it must boil over."

In the 1830s, it did. Peasants began to attack landlords, burning their property, threatening and beating their agents. One band of desperate cotters crept into an estate at midnight and plowed up the land so the landlord could not use it for grazing. Throughout Ireland, the number of fires, assaults, and murders rose higher and higher. Mary's father and grandfather were both caught up in the wild and defiant actions of the rebellious peasants.

The elder Mr. Harris joined one of the underground societies the peasants formed to fight against the landlords. A solemn, brawny man, he was used to spending his days working the land and his evenings in his son's cottage with his infant granddaughter Mary on his lap. Now he and the other peasants put on hoods and masks and went out at night, armed with pitchforks and knives. They set fire to cottages from which tenants had been evicted. They ambushed and beat estate managers, summons servers, and rent collectors.

The British government, which ruled all of Ireland, declared a state of emergency and sent soldiers to occupy the countryside. They made sweeping arrests of all those known or thought to be members of an underground group. Marching the prisoners single file along the stony roads, the soldiers herded them into makeshift jails, pens, and lean-to's. When Mary was two years old, her grandfather was arrested in a massive sweep of southern County Cork. He was imprisoned under military law and hung.

Mary was very young when these things happened. But they left their mark on her. Even as an old woman, she remembered with horror the spring morning when soldiers came marching down the dusty road to her village. There were cries and screams from the peasants who saw them—for on the soldiers' bayonets were the severed heads of rebel peasants.

Mary also remembered the day her father told them he would have to flee. The year was 1835. A relentlessly rainy spring had followed a rainy fall and winter. Crops rotted in the ground. Some of the Harrises' neighbors were starving. Others saw their cottages melt away like sugar in the torrential downpours. Mary's father joined his neighbors in an underground group which terrorized landlords, stole stores of food, raided military encampments and freed the peasants imprisoned there. Then his identity

An illustration of an Irish cotter's home in the early 1800s.

was learned and his name was placed on a "wanted" list. He was to be captured, the edict said, and hung.

Soon after Richard Harris learned of the list, soldiers appeared at his cottage. Mary's young brothers were asleep, but the five-year-old girl stood beside her mother as the soldiers pounded on the door, demanding that Richard Harris come out.

Mary's mother called to the soldiers that her husband was not there.

They did not believe her. Coming inside, they scoured the cottage from roof to floor, tearing down even the chimney as Mary watched from behind her mother's skirts. But the soldiers did not find him.

According to one account, Mary's father escaped on a fishing boat. Local fishermen might very well have been willing to help someone who was running from the law, for antigovernment feelings were so common in Ireland that it was sometimes said that all Irishmen were "outlaws."

Where the fishing boat deposited Richard Harris and how he made his way to America are not known. But get to America he did. In September his family received word from him. He was safe in New York; he had found work—and he would send for them as soon as he saved the money for their passage and found them a place to live.

The next time Mary saw her father she was eleven years old and had traveled 3,000 miles across the ocean in a battered, crowded immigrant ship called *The William.* Neither she nor her brothers, Sean and Shamus, recognized Richard Harris, standing near the gangplank, scanning the faces of the ragged people coming ashore. They might have walked on by had not their mother suddenly put her bundles down and rushed forward to embrace him.

From the time he arrived in America, Richard had worked as a laborer. Like thousands of other Irish immigrants, he had been hired "on the dock" for a job few native Americans cared to take: construction work on the great canal systems being built in the northeastern states. It was crude, hard labor with pick and ax, but it was steady work and the immigrants were glad to have it.

They lived in camps pitched beside the excavations, beginning their work at sunrise and ending at sunset. The pay was seventy-five cents a day in the summer, when days were long, fifty cents in winter. These were low wages, even by the standards of the 1830s, but better than anything that could have been found in Ireland. If a man was thrifty, as Richard Harris was, he could put some money aside each week, even if it was only pennies. In fact, many of the immigrants at work on canals did just that. Thirty thousand people were arriving from Ireland every year, most of them helped by a friend or relative who had gone before. "Give us but the means," one Irishman said, "and half the country will go."

After five years in America, Richard had "the means" to bring his family over. In the spring of 1841, he made arrangements with the captain of a ship soon to depart for Ireland. It would unload its cargo in Cork harbor and pick up passengers for the return trip to New York.

The captain could not give Richard the exact date of the ship's sailing because in those days schedules depended on the weather. Ships remained in the harbor waiting to depart until there were "fair winds." The crossing itself could vary by more than a month. In good weather, a well-fitted ship could make it in four weeks. But if there were storms at sea or bad winds, the crossing could take ten weeks. Mrs. Harris would have to prepare herself and the children and then watch for the shipping company's announcement of *The William*'s arrival.

When the notice appeared in the Cork *Weekly Register* on the second of September, Mrs. Harris and the children were ready. There was little to pack. Most of what they carried was food—since the ship did not provide the passengers with anything but water during the crossing. The agent at the dock told Mrs. Harris that repairs were being made which would take two or three days, and then they would be off "with the first fair winds."

Mary spent her last days in Ireland in a rooming house, one of the many that lined the streets near the docks. She and her mother and brothers shared a room with another family also waiting to leave. All of them rationed their provisions carefully, for the food would have to last until they landed in America.

Finally, *The William* was ready to sail. The immigrants, boxes and bundles and babies in tow, were shepherded to their quarters and left to make do as best they could. Mrs. Harris set her provisions down and spread blankets on the floor for herself and the children to sleep on. All about them, other families were doing the same.

According to British regulations, there was supposed to be five feet of deck space for each passenger aboard an ocean-going vessel. But *The William*, like most immigrant ships, carried as many people as could be crowded aboard. They were quartered in every available nook and cranny and on special platforms built "between decks." Mary's mother remained below in the cramped space and stale air for almost the entire voyage, for the top decks were continually swept by the cold gray waves of the North Atlantic. Mary's brother Sean was ill day after day from the tossing and tilting of the small ship in the rough sea. Many passengers could do little more than sleep or try to sleep and wait for the time when they would reach land.

On the fourth of October, the 3,000-mile journey ended. The passengers of *The William* had been at sea for seven weeks. An observer on the pier that day would surely have seen relief—and hope—on the faces of many of those who stepped ashore.

Perhaps he would not have noticed the skinny young girl who hesitated for a moment at the head of the gangplank. But even if he had, he would surely not have imagined that she would be a famous woman one day, that she would dine with Presidents and defy presidential orders, or confer with millionaires and tell them they had no right to their money.

"I belong to a class," Mary Harris would say in years to come, when asked to explain her actions to a committee from the Congress of the United States, "I belong to a class which has been robbed, exploited, and plundered down through many long centuries. And because I belong to that class, I have an impulse to go and help break the chains."

For the other passengers leaving *The William* that day, what was probably the most difficult journey of their lives was over. For Mary Harris, the journey had just begun.

~ TWO ~

GROWING UP, GOING AWAY

The Harris family settled in Toronto, Canada, for that was where Richard's work had taken him. When construction on the canals was finished, Richard had gone to work for the railroad on a crew which was based in Toronto. There, plans for a new line were being made.

When the Harrises arrived in the fall of 1841, Toronto was a city on the move. Ten years earlier, it had been called "York," and was described as a "dirty, straggling village," "a little, ill-built town" on the forest path between the Don River and Lake Ontario. But soon the town of York became the incorporated city of Toronto, and Toronto became the capital of the Province of Upper Canada. Stores, churches, and public buildings went up. New streets and avenues were laid. Charles Dickens visited Toronto the same year the Harrises arrived and called it "a town full of life and motion, bustle, business and improvement." It had roads finished with macadam. It had shops with plate-glass windows. It had a town hall, a college, a courthouse, row after row of brick buildings roofed with tin, and a thriving harbor lined with wharves. The citizens of Toronto, especially those who had been there since the days when it was known as "muddy little York," were still a bit awed by the growth. To the Harrises, the city was spectacular.

Gaslights were installed in 1841, before the Harrises arrived—one hundred lamps on King Street, each with the power of ten candles. Residents came by the hundreds on the crisp December evening when the lights were turned on for the first time. It was considered a dazzling display. Mary was no less dazzled when she first saw them lighting up the long avenue, lovelier than any star.

The Harrises lived in a small frame house, and according to census records, Mr. Harris "owned 2 pigs: value, $40." Though the pigs were kept in the backyard and could be heard—and smelled—from every corner of the two-room house, they were the pride of the immigrant family from Ireland. There, anyone who owned a pig had been the envy of his neighbors.

Mr. Harris earned a dollar a day—enough so that, according to Mary, the family lived "without luxuries but also without wants." A very good house in Toronto could be rented for one hundred dollars a year. A pound of beef cost a nickel, a dozen eggs cost ten cents. His job secure, his family housed and fed, Mr. Harris felt that he had a great deal to be thankful for.

Mary and her brothers found friends among the other immigrant families who arrived in great numbers every month. When their household chores were done, they were free to wander, and Toronto was filled with places to fascinate and delight them.

The outskirts of the city—fields, forests, and the lovely Don

River—were a short walk from the Harrises' house. The harbor was a stone's throw in the other direction. On a summer's day, they might see ships from Europe unloading at the wharves. In winter, the frozen harbor itself became a playground for the children who slid and skated on it until dark. And every evening, just at dusk, they could follow the town crier as he made his rounds calling out the descriptions of lost animals, lost children, or the details of the latest accident or crime.

The Harrises had been in the city for about two years when free public schools opened for the first time. The wealthier people had long sent their children to exclusive—and expensive—private

Toronto as it looked during Mary's youth.

schools, or had arranged for private tutors at home. The new "common" schools—as elementary schools were called—would provide an education for the poorer children of the city. Attendance was not compulsory, and the majority did not enroll. But Mary's parents, though barely able to read and write themselves, sent their children to school.

Only the basic skills—reading, writing, and arithmetic—were taught. That was enough to persuade Mary's parents the schools were worthwhile. But that is also about the best that can be said for them. The buildings were primitive, often one-room log structures, heated by a fire which the teacher built. Classes were

enormous—75 to 100 children in each. One teacher complained that in his class, children of all ages were "packed in their seats as close as one's fingers, and were equally in danger of suffocating as of freezing to death." Because of the large classes, the "monitorial" system was used. The teacher worked only with the older or more advanced students, and they in turn worked with the younger or less advanced. But even the teachers themselves were not trained. The ability to read and write was the only requirement for the job, and most teachers did not consider their positions permanent. For men, it was something to do while they were between other jobs. For women, who had very few job options, it was something to do until marriage.

Discipline was fierce, imposed by teacher and monitor alike with a heavy hand. Sticks and sometimes whips were used to punish children who disobeyed the rules. And there were rules to cover almost everything—from the way to sit, to the way to raise a pencil.

Difficult as it was to "shine" in a school situation like that, Mary did. She was an excellent student, advanced quickly, and was soon a monitor. She enjoyed working with the younger children and began to think she might become a teacher herself one day. Her parents took great pride in her accomplishments. Though they sent Mary's brothers to work when they completed common school, Mary was encouraged to go on to high school. She became the first high-school graduate in the Harris family.

In 1847, in an attempt to improve the common school system, a normal school—a training school for teachers—was opened in Toronto. Mary wanted to apply for admission when she graduated from high school. But when the school first opened, it did not accept women. Some people urged the superintendent to make it a "coeducational" institution—something almost unheard of in those days. The superintendent said he would consider it. In the meantime, Mary remained at home. She learned the fundamentals of dressmaking from her mother, and soon was an accomplished seamstress. She could design clothing as well as copy existing garments. Within a few months, she was taking orders from friends and neighbors and earning a small income as a seamstress.

Mary was not the only woman who had wished to be trained as a teacher, and the barriers to their acceptance in training schools soon began to come down. In the Province of New Brunswick, a young woman named Martha Hamm Lewis had applied to the new normal school there and had been rejected because the school did not accept "females." But Martha kept reapplying, attaching to her application arguments against the school's admission policy. Finally, in 1849, she was accepted—under certain conditions: she had to enter the classroom ten minutes before the other students, and she was required to wear a veil. She had to sit alone at the back of the room, and leave five minutes before the lecture ended without speaking to any of the male students.

Mary did not have to go through that. While Martha Lewis was challenging the barriers against women in New Brunswick, the Toronto Normal School officially opened its doors to women. In the first year, twenty-one students were enrolled in the new "female department." Soon after that, Mary applied and was admitted.

The work in the program was staggering. Students attended lectures for nine hours a day and then put in one hour of observation and practice teaching at a model school. One critic of the system complained that after such training, it was no surprise that graduates became "slave drivers" to the children they taught.

Mary finished the first year of the two-year program at the Toronto Normal School. She was admitted to the second session, but her name does not appear on the list of those who completed it. So evidently she did not graduate. But at a time when most teachers had no training at all, one year's training was more than enough to qualify her for any position she might wish to hold.

Mary was, however, disqualified from teaching in the Toronto common schools for an entirely different reason: her religion. Mary and her family were Roman Catholic, and though they were not observant—Mary, in fact, would always be more a critic of the Church than a friend—nevertheless, at that time there was an unwritten law against hiring Roman Catholics, observant or otherwise.

Perhaps that is the reason why, less than a year later, Mary left Canada. But something else may have happened too, something which perhaps strained the relationship between the twenty-two-year-old woman and her family. For until this time, there is every reason to believe that they got along well. But once Mary left Toronto, as far as anyone knows, she never saw her family again. If they exchanged letters, no record of them remains. Neither in her autobiography nor in any public statement that Mary ever made did she mention her family or indicate that she was in touch with them. What, if anything, happened to account for this remains a mystery.

From Canada, Mary went to Maine, where she worked as a private tutor. Not much is known about her situation there, but if it was a typical one, she lived with the family whose children she taught and had complete responsibility for their education. Though conditions were usually pleasant enough—the tutor was given a private room and treated as a respected member of the family—most of the young people who took these jobs did not stay more than one or two years. Mary was no exception. In 1857, two years after her arrival, she was off again, this time to a job as a teacher in a Catholic school, St. Mary's, in Monroe, Michigan. But Mary chafed under the strict discipline with which the school was run—from the early curfews and bed-checks to the assigned seating at the breakfast table. She also disliked having to be a strict disciplinarian—and this, she felt, was all the school really wanted of its teachers.

In the spring of 1858, Mary collected her year's wages—$36.40, low even when room and board are taken into account—and left for Chicago. She had decided to try her hand as a dressmaker. Many years later, in her *Autobiography*—a book that isn't always accurate about dates and places, but always presents a clear account of Mary's feelings—she explained her move in one short but revealing sentence: "I thought I would prefer sewing to bossing little children."

THREE

MARRIAGE

Mary stayed in Chicago for only two years. According to some accounts, she found it very difficult to earn a living as a seamstress. But in any case, the desire to teach had remained with her— if she could find a place that allowed her to teach in the way she wished.

In the spring of 1860, she learned of the need for teachers in Memphis, Tennessee. Hoping that there she would be able to find a position that suited her, Mary left for Memphis in the summer to look around and, if luck was with her, find a place before the new fall term.

Situated on a bluff overlooking the Mississippi, Memphis was the Queen of the River between St. Louis and New Orleans. Its wharves were lined with steamboats, and its railroad tracks pushed out like fingers into the rich farmlands to the south. High-spirited and frontier in flavor, it had attracted thousands of newcomers—immigrants and native-born Americans alike—and had grown from a town of 1,800 people to a city of over 20,000 in just twenty years. In fact, it was because of the tremendous growth during the 1840s and 1850s that Memphis had accomplished what no other southern city had done—established a public school system, free of cost and open to all. In 1860, when Mary arrived, other southern cities were just beginning to set up free public schools. Memphis already had twenty-one and an annual enrollment of almost 2,000 children. Experienced and well-trained, Mary easily found work.

Like many of the poorer newcomers to Memphis, Mary lived in a section known on the map as Catfish Bay. People in Memphis called it "Pinchgut" or "Pinch" because, so the story goes, the people who lived there were "so poor that their guts were always pinched." Pinch was indeed a slum, with its small frame houses ringing the tepid, semi-stagnant waters of the bay. Though the inhabitants claimed not to notice, the smell of dead fish filled the air and drove visitors wild. Nevertheless, it was the best Mary could afford. She rented rooms in a boarding house and began to prepare for the class she would teach when the schools opened in October.

Memphis, in addition to being a steamboat, railroad, and cotton center, was also a foundry town. The Memphis Iron Works, in the north end, turned out hatchets, horseshoes, plows, stoves, and, most important of all, tracks for the growing railroad industry. The key workers in the foundry were the molders, highly skilled men who melted down the iron in huge furnaces and poured it into molds. One of the molders was a tall, thin man named George Jones. He was the man Mary would marry.

George was a native of Tennessee, born in the rugged moun-

A view of Memphis as it looked in 1860, when Mary arrived.

tains in the eastern part of the state. He had come to Memphis because of the exciting opportunities the growing city seemed to offer. He had never been to school, but he had taught himself to read and write. He was strong, soft-spoken, and hard-working.

George earned a good salary as an iron molder, but he had to work six days a week, from eight in the morning until nine at night to get it—in a workshop where open furnaces blazed fiercely and filled the air with smoke and steam.

Soon after he went to work in the foundry, George and a group of other molders approached the owners to talk about the conditions under which they worked—particularly the heat, which

26

in summer made the shop a serious menace to health. But the owners would not see them, and the men knew that if they protested further, they would be fired.

Many of the molders felt that they were helpless. They would have to accept conditions as they were, since there was nothing they could do to change them. George did not agree. He had heard that a union for molders existed. It was in fact one of the first unions to be created in the United States. Begun in Philadelphia in the 1850s by a molder named William Sylvus, the National Union of Iron Molders was pledged to improving conditions for all molders—shortening the work day, ventilating the shops, protecting the workers' health and safety. But most important of all, the union's leaders looked forward to the day when workers would be treated with respect—when they would have a voice in the management of the shops in which they labored.

Though the other molders were only vaguely—if at all—aware of the union and its goals, George was excited about it. By nature he was a quiet man, but he took it upon himself to talk to the other workers about the union and to urge them to work with him in establishing a local branch.

Serious, warm-hearted and committed to a dream, George met Mary sometime in the fall of 1860. They seem to have fallen in love almost as soon as they met, for within two months they were married. The Joneses rented a large old house on the outskirts of Pinch, but they hardly had time to settle down before Memphis was filled with talk of rebellion and Civil War. In December, shortly after their wedding, Abraham Lincoln was inaugurated President of the United States. Immediately, South Carolina withdrew from the Union, and shortly thereafter the other six states of the Deep South announced their secession.

The issue of secession raged in Tennessee, where the people were deeply divided. Memphis itself was the scene of pro-Union as well as anti-Union activities. There might be a demonstration calling for secession one night, then a rally in support of the Union the next. George and Mary were committed to the Union side, and together they attended rallies and demonstrations in its behalf.

Then in April, Confederate guns fired on Fort Sumter, in South Carolina. The fort fell. Two days later, President Lincoln issued a general call-to-arms. The Union Army would march on South Carolina, take back the fort, and put down the rebels.

Bonfires blazed on Memphis' main streets when news reached the city. Torchlight parades were held in several sections. "Come one, come all," the marchers yelled. "Come one, come all who are against northern aggression." Now the people of Tennessee closed ranks with the people in the other southern states. "The Union is beyond salvation," the governor of Tennessee said. "Our only choice is to join a northern Confederacy or a southern one." The state legislature called a special meeting to debate the issue and to vote.

There was no doubt what the outcome of the vote would be— and in fact the people of Memphis did not hesitate to begin their preparations on behalf of the South. Steamers in the harbor were forced to take down the American flag and to raise the flag of the southern Confederacy. The city militia began drilling in the streets. "War fever" had come to Memphis.

For almost a year, from June, 1861, until May, 1862, Memphis was, in the words of one journalist, "a wild war town." The whistles of enormous steamers could be heard night and day, while

the bells of heavy supply trains sounded in the distance. For-
tifications were built on the bluff. Hotels swarmed with army officers. The people were high-spirited, cheerful, and enthusiastic
about a war which they thought would be quickly and gloriously
won. No one could publicly support the Union now.

George and Mary followed the news in silence, hoping to hear
of Union victories. They did not wish to betray their friends and
neighbors, but they believed that the northern side was the right
side. In their private lives, however, they had reason to be very
happy. For in January of 1862 their first child was born.

In the spring, after a year of war, Memphis' enthusiasm was
replaced by sadness and weariness. Northern troops had captured
a fort on the river just above the city, and supply lines leading into
Memphis had been cut off.

There was no safe way into the city, and no way out. There was
no meat, no coffee, no clothing, books, or fuel. Shops, even those
on the main streets, closed at two. Almost daily, hundreds of
wounded soldiers were brought into the city, which became, as
one Memphian said, a "vast hospital."

The authorities began to prepare for the capture of Memphis,
for now defeat seemed almost inevitable. Thousands of bales of
cotton were hauled to the outskirts of town and set on fire, so the
Union would not be able to use them. Barrels of molasses were
taken to the riverbank, their heads knocked off, and the contents
allowed to ooze down into the mud. Sugar barrels were over-
turned and the sugar scattered in the dirt.

Memphis would be a great prize to the North. With it, the
Union would control the Mississippi River. And Memphis' net-
work of railroads, in combination with the river, would make it an
ideal base for supplies and troops for the North, just as it had been

for the South. But Memphis had sent 4,000 young soldiers off to war. Almost 2,000 had already been killed. For most of the people in the city, the end of the war could not come soon enough.

Then, on the sixth of June, a day which dawned beautiful and clear, Yankee gunboats were sighted below the bluff. Word spread quickly through the city. Thousands of people gathered on the cliff to watch as the Confederate boats which guarded Memphis—steamers and gunboats—formed a double line around the base of the city.

The Union fleet was in full view now: eight gunboats and a dozen steel rams, tugs, and transports. Soon they were within range of the Confederate ships, and the Confederates opened fire. At that, two Yankee rams came speeding forward. They crashed into the Confederate boats while Yankee sharpshooters on the gunboats which followed the rams picked off Confederate pilots. The battle was over in a little more than an hour. The city of Memphis surrendered, and the Confederate flag flying over the courthouse was lowered and put away.

George volunteered to serve in the Union Army, but he was turned down because his eyesight was poor. He continued to work as a molder, happy to be aiding the Union side rather than the Confederate, for molders were important to the war effort. He would have to wait for the end of the war, however, to resume his efforts to build a local branch of the Molders Union. Even the main body of the union in Philadelphia had dissolved with the coming of war, since leaders and members alike had been called to fight, and those who stayed behind were too caught up in production to keep a union active.

The Northern Army occupied Memphis for four years, but it

was not a harsh occupation. A curfew was imposed—after mid-night anyone found in alleys, byways, or "unusual places" was locked up until morning. Aside from that, the people of Memphis did not suffer under Yankee rule. Industry, which had boomed when the war began, but fallen sharply when Memphis' supply lines were cut off, now was going full steam once again. There was little resistance to the occupying forces. If anything, things were better than they had been before the war began.

George and Mary lived quietly and comfortably. They were

Citizens thronging the Memphis Courthouse as the Union flag is raised.

certain that the North would win in the end, that unions would be established once the war was over, and that conditions for working people would improve. Three more children were born to them by the time peace was declared in 1865.

With peace came a new era of prosperity for Memphis. Tons of cotton, the "white gold" of the Delta, were brought to its wharves and depots daily, and the world was eager to buy it. Soon Memphis was second only to New Orleans in business activity. Production in the foundries was up, since railroads, beginning to reach all the way across the continent, depended on the foundries for tracks and cars.

George returned to the work he cared about most: organizing a Memphis branch of the Iron Molders Union. Six months after the end of the war, Memphis Local No. 66 was officially chartered. George's dream had begun to come true.

Organizing had picked up in other parts of the nation too. In 1860, the union had had 1,000 members. In 1867, it had 8,615. Soon the Iron Molders Union was able to pay salaries to the people who wanted to work for it. George became a full-time organizer, traveling throughout Tennessee and into the surrounding states, talking to workers, explaining what the union was, and urging them to join. Mary followed his work, and came to believe that unions were the answer to the problems of the working people. She didn't travel with him, but she encouraged him and made him feel free to come and go as the work demanded—even though that meant she was without him for weeks at a stretch. Still, there was not much time for her to be lonely with four healthy young children to care for. Life was full and very good for the Joneses as 1866 drew to a close.

᨞ FOUR ᨞

PLAGUE AND FIRE

Yellow fever! The very name was enough to strike terror into people's hearts. A disease which came without warning, spread like the wind, and left death behind. What caused it, how to cure it, how to prevent it, no one living could say for certain. Now, yellow fever came to Memphis.

The rains had begun early in the spring of 1867, heavier and more constant than had fallen in many years. People muttered about the clogged streets and muddy roads, especially in areas like Pinch which, though it had almost doubled in population during the war, was still without an adequate drainage system, without sewers, without a reliable source of fresh water. Pools and puddles collected and grew larger. When the rains ended, and the sun baked down, mosquitoes seemed to be everywhere. Among them were the mosquitoes that, unknown to people at the time, carried yellow fever.

The first death occurred in August. The symptoms were unmistakable. First the victim experienced chills and fever and pain in the head and back. The next day the victim would seem to be better, but his skin would take on a yellowish tinge. Then the yellow would become mottled with black. Finally, in the last and most awful stage, the victim would be unable to hold down food and would erupt with black vomit. His body would give off a horrible stench that some people compared to the smell of rotten hay; others said the odor was just indescribable. For most people, death followed a day or two later.

As soon as word of the fever's presence got out, people began to leave the city. Wagons and carriages jammed the roads leading to the railroad depots and steamboat landings. Trunks were hurriedly packed and piled onto carts which clanked swiftly out of town. Within the week, the only people left in the city were either too poor to leave or had no place to go.

No one knew who would be struck next. No one knew what to do to help. The chairman of the New Orleans Board of Health, then the leading authority on epidemic diseases, said, "The yellow fever must run its course, and nothing that we know of can stop it."

By September, hardly a household remained untouched. Memphis was filled with death and the cries of the dying, and the town took on the rhythm of the plague. By day, doctors, nurses, priests, and nuns rushed from one patient to another. They tried everything. Holding rags and sponges to their noses, they washed the victims with disinfectants, gave them hot baths, covered them with ice packs, wrapped them in blankets dipped in hot water. They sponged them, fanned them, gave them castor oil, tea, wine. They did anything that any doctor anywhere had ever suggested.

By night, an awful stillness settled on the town, and life itself seemed suspended. The only sounds were the tread of a policeman on his beat, the shrieks of someone in the delirium of the fever, and the death bell tolling in the cemetery.

A nun visits a poor household that has been stricken with yellow fever.

The city authorities tried to "contain" the plague. Churches, schools, and all the places where people gathered were closed. Windows and doors were ordered shut and sealed against the "bad air." Houses in which the plague had entered were quarantined; no one could enter without official permission.

Streets and sidewalks were soaked in disinfectant and carbolic acid. Lime was sprinkled on damp patches of ground until the city seemed to be covered with snowdrifts. Barrels of tar were rolled into the streets and set on fire. And on every sidewalk could be seen flaming piles of mattresses and bedclothes which had belonged to people who had died. Day and night, the city was blanketed in smoke.

But the plague continued. "The dead surrounded us," Mary later wrote. "All about my house I could hear weeping and the cries of delirium." Every morning, just before dawn, the grating sounds of the death wagon could be heard, touring the streets to collect the bodies. "Bring out your dead," called the drivers, hooded and masked, as the horses clattered down the silent streets.

Catherine, five years old, was the first of Mary's children to die. Then Terence, two, and Elizabeth, three, were dead. The next week, the first week in October, Mary stood in her doorway and looked at the dawn, her last child, barely a year old, dead in her arms. "One by one my four little children sickened and died," she wrote. "I washed their little bodies and got them ready for burial."

George was stricken and died in the week that followed. Two days later, on the fifteenth of October, the Memphis chapter of the Iron Molders Union held a meeting in his honor. The charter was draped in mourning, and the following notice appeared in the Iron Molders' *Journal.*

MEMPHIS, TENN., *October 20, 1867.*

At a special meeting of Iron Molders' Union, No. 66, held October 15th, 1867, the following preamble and resolutions were unanimously adopted in respect to the memory of our departed brother, George E. Jones:

Whereas, It has pleased Almighty God, in his infinite wisdom, to remove by death, after a short but painful illness, an earnest and energetic brother; therefore be it

Resolved, That we truly sympathize with the widow and relatives of our deceased brother, and offer our condolence for their irreparable loss in this world; hoping that God may reveal that all things work together for our good.

Resolved, That our charter be draped in mourning for thirty days.

Resolved, That a copy of these resolutions be presented to his widow and other relatives, and also be published in the daily papers of this city and I. M. I. JOURNAL.

The local paid the funeral expenses of George as it had for his four children.

At first Mary prayed that she too would be taken. But something, perhaps the very grief she was experiencing and the suffering her own family had gone through, impelled her to go and try to help the others. A few days after burying her husband, Mary got a permit to enter quarantined homes and nurse the victims. In one cottage, she found a woman with a baby in her arms. The woman was walking the floor and singing a lullaby. She neither saw nor heard Mary as she let herself into the room. The baby had been dead for hours. In another house, a woman was sitting in a rocking chair, dead, with a dead child on her lap. On the floor beside the chair, a second child lay dying.

There was not much anyone could do to comfort the victims and their families. Mary bathed the ill, fed those who could eat, sat with them, took care of the children whose parents were sick or dying.

The people knew that the plague would be over when the weather turned cold, although they didn't know why. So the stricken city waited for the first heavy frost. In December, it came, and the yellow fever epidemic ended. As Memphis counted its dead, and the survivors began to rebuild their lives, Mary made plans to leave the city. She decided to go back to Chicago and make her way alone.

The members of George's union collected money for Mary. It was not much, for they did not have much, but it would keep her going for a little while. Mary said she would work as a seamstress again.

The city Mary found when she arrived in Chicago in the winter of 1868 was the largest, busiest city in the Midwest. Chicago had grown with incredible speed during the Civil War, because it was an ideal center for the trade and shipping that was so essential. On the east side, Chicago touched Lake Michigan, one of the Great Lakes and part of a natural waterway between east and west. To the south, north, and west of Chicago were fertile plains on which grain, hogs, steer, and sheep were raised. Sixty-five million bushels of grain a year had been shipped from Chicago to the troops during the war. One third of all the meat the Union purchased was slaughtered and packed and shipped from Chicago. Railroad construction boomed, and twenty-one major lines were routed through Chicago—making it the "crossroads of the nation." Over 200 trains entered and left the city daily. The population grew until there were almost 200,000 people by the end of the war, and Chicago had added twenty-four square miles to its boundaries.

Many Chicagoans became millionaires. Among them were Marshall Field, who owned and operated the celebrated Marshall Field department store; Phillip Armour, the "king of meat-packing"; his arch rival, Gustavus Franklin Swift; and Cyrus McCormick, described in the newspapers as "the hot-tempered Mr. Bang," who invented a farm reaper and then opened his own factory in Chicago. All these men—and others besides—were millionaires many times over by the end of the Civil War. In fact, the entire nation had plunged into a heady—some said hysterical— love affair with money. There were fortunes to be made, and many people who were determined to make them. Wealth seemed to be the highest goal of life, and it was considered unnecessary to worry about the methods used to obtain it—or who might be hurt in the process.

"Get money, honestly if you can—but at any rate get money!" That was society's message, said Henry George, a political re- former who thought the "money fever" was destroying people's sense of honor and America's tradition of justice.

Other people did not agree. Wasn't America the land of oppor- tunity, where everyone had the chance to become rich? They be- lieved those who succeeded were fulfilling the nation's promise and confirming its belief in the power of the individual. Some even claimed that the wealthy had been singled out and blessed. "I believe the power to make money is the gift of God," said John D. Rockefeller, Jr., whose father, the founder of the family fortune, explained in humbler terms how he taught his children to be successful. "I cheat my boys every time I get a chance," he said once. "I want to make 'em sharp."

Even the wealthiest of the new industrialists paid their employees as little as they could. To do otherwise would have gone against their belief that profits and wealth were the most important things of all. And besides, they claimed, anyone who was "worth anything" would find a way to work his way up from the bottom. Those who remained poor deserved their fate. The Reverend Russell H. Conwell suggested that the poor were being punished by God. "To sympathize with a man whom God has punished for his sins is to do wrong, no doubt about it," he said, in a speech so popular that he took it on tour and presented it to almost 6,000 audiences throughout the country during the 1870s. "There is not a poor person in the United States who was not made poor by his own shortcomings or by the shortcomings of someone else," Conwell concluded. "It is all wrong to be poor."

Sinners or victims, the poor were everywhere. Nowhere was the contrast between them and the wealthy more evident than in Chicago, which, Mary noted, had become a "divided city." In the northeast, beside the lake, the people lived graciously and comfortably. Most of the homes were mansions—some were palaces. Cyrus McCormick's massive sandstone home not only had a different room for every occasion—a music room, a reading room, a sitting room, a tea room, a breakfast room, and others—it also had two libraries, a master library and a grand library, decorated in ebony inlaid with silver, and a private theater which could hold 200 people.

The Palmer residence, one of many elegant mansions built in Chicago in the 1870s.

On the south and west sides, amid the new factories and slaughterhouses which sent foul stenches into the air, was "poor Chicago." Here people lived in crowded, sunless tenements and ramshackle wooden frame houses. Whole families lived in one or two rooms. In the narrow side yards some people kept chickens and, if they could afford to buy one, a cow. Row after row of shacks, tenements, and sheds stretched to the very edge of the prairie.

Children of the poor in Chicago. They were often badly nourished and ill.

When Mary arrived in Chicago, she found a storefront shop in the west end. It was cheap, and it had a room in the back where she could sleep. Skilled at her trade, she was soon earning a small yet adequate income. But the contrast between the rich and the poor disturbed her.

Mary's customers were the wealthy people of Chicago. Often, she worked in their houses, carefully fitting the ladies in gorgeous gowns, or stitching elaborate draperies and elegant covers for their fine couches and chairs. As she sewed, she thought of the working people on the other side of town.

Fifty years later, in her *Autobiography,* Mary described how she felt in those days.

> Often while sewing for the lords and barons who dwelt in magnificent houses along the Lake Shore Drive, I would look out the windows and see the poor, shivering wretches, jobless and hungry, walking along the frozen lake front. The contrast of their condition with that of the tropical comfort of the people for whom I sewed was painful to me. My employers seemed neither to notice nor to care.

In summer, too, the poor suffered while the rich escaped to country homes and mountain resorts.

"I used to watch the mothers, come from the west side slums," Mary wrote, "lugging babies and little children, hoping for a breath of cool, fresh air from the lake. At night, when the tenements were stifling hot, men, women and little children slept in the parks."

From time to time, Mary met people who had known her husband, iron molders and other workers. From them she learned that the Molders Union, though still alive, had come upon hard times. It was being fought tooth and nail by foundry owners. They were keeping "blacklists"—lists of people who belonged to the union. People on the lists were fired and replaced with non-union workers, and there was nothing anyone could do about it. Nothing—except, as one molder said, to keep recruiting new members until the day when all molders were in the union. And in fact, hard as it was, and hopeless as it sometimes seemed, the union in the late 1860s was growing.

Chicago continued to grow, too, faster than any other city in the United States. Since timber was plentiful and cheap, almost everything was made of wood. Blocks of small wooden houses, shacks, barns, and sheds pushed the city limits outward in all directions. Out of the seventy streets which were surfaced at all, fifty-five were surfaced with pine blocks, fitted into the roadways as if they were bricks. Sidewalks, raised above the ground to prevent mud from seeping through, were also made of wood. Fences made of pine or hemlock ran along most streets and between lots. The trains in yards and stations throughout the city were made largely of wood, as were the seventeen grain elevators on the west side. They stood, five stories high, like torches waiting to be ignited. In the business districts, the warehouses and stores were full of wooden shelves and cases. And, since Chicago was becoming a center of woodworking industries, furniture factories rose beside lumber mills, carriage and wagon works beside paint and varnish shops. All the industries depended on steam power, so their yards were piled high with coal for their boilers. Chicago was ripe for burning.

The people were aware that fire was their most dangerous enemy, so careful defenses were set up against it. Fire towers, rising high above the city's buildings, dotted the landscape. The towers were staffed around the clock by watchmen whose job was to spot smoke and flames and signal the nearest firehouse immediately. Chicago's firefighters were the best trained in the country, and its fire-fighting equipment was the best then available. It had seventeen "steamers"—horse-drawn carriages equipped with boilers to power steam-driven pumps.

The spring and summer of 1871 were hot and dry, even for Chicago. By the end of August, almost every night fire bells could be heard ringing somewhere in the distance. Fires always drew crowds of people, especially children, for they were exciting spectacles. But Mary, like most veteran Chicagoans, barely noticed the fire bells. They seemed to be just another sound in the city, part of the day, part of the night. She did not pay much attention to the bells on the night of Sunday, October 7, though there were many that evening. In a barn on the west side, a cow had kicked over a lantern. The hay caught fire, and the barn began to burn. The wooden fence lining the street carried the fire down the block. Then the sidewalks began to burn, and then the houses. The Great Chicago Fire had begun.

A watchman in a fire tower saw the flames but misjudged their location. He gave the wrong signal, and a fire company in a district far from the blaze went racing out. The mistake gave the fire a head-start, and the wind did the rest. Suddenly picking up and sweeping through the city from the north, the wind fanned the fire, sending sheets of flame billowing through the air to streets it might never have reached otherwise. An observer said that once the fire was underway, the firemen could no more have put it out than they could have put out the wind. Michael Conway, a firefighter on the scene, said, "I do not think it could have been stopped unless you picked it up and threw it into the lake."

People poured out of their houses. If they had valuable possessions, they buried them in the ground before they fled.

Mary's block was evacuated just before dawn. Taking only a sack of food, she joined the crowds moving toward safe ground at the shore of Lake Michigan. She lost everything she owned in the fire. Homeless once again, she camped at the lake with 30,000 others.

The fire raged out of control for three days. It destroyed 100,000 homes in an area one mile wide and four miles long, one sixth of Chicago. "There was not a sound to break the solitude," an observer wrote, "not a building to change the blackened landscape. Wood was reduced to dust and all metals shrank away in liquid rivulets and disappeared."

For a day and a night the campers at the lakeshore had no food. They shared what few things they had been able to bring with them. Then contributions from people in nearby towns began to arrive. Mary helped to distribute food, while in the distance the fire sent up columns of smoke and flame.

By Friday, food and clothing for the refugees began to arrive from people all over the United States. The city government set up distribution centers in churches and schools, and Mary volunteered to work in a kitchen. When public buildings and churches were opened as dormitories, Mary took shelter in the basement of St. Mary's Church.

In the evenings, when others were busy with their families, Mary sometimes walked through the burned-out district. Everything was gone. Where her shop had stood there was now only rubble. Who could tell how long it would take to rebuild all that had been destroyed? For most of the wealthy people, the losses would soon be made up. If their homes were gone, they would

The intersection of Jackson and State streets, after the fire. One-sixth of the city was destroyed.

build new ones. They had insurance, resources, credit, and connections. But the poor had nothing.

One evening as Mary was out walking, she discovered, in a fire-scorched building that looked all but abandoned, a meeting of a secret organization of workers: the Noble and Holy Order of the Knights of Labor. The Knights had to keep their meetings secret because they would be fired from their jobs if their employers learned that they were members.

Mary was walking by the building where the meeting was being held when she saw a man she knew from Memphis, an iron molder who had worked with her husband. He was standing at the door, on the alert for anyone who might "crash" the meeting. Mary chatted with him, and he invited her to go inside and see what they were doing.

The Knights were idealists. They wanted every working person in the United States—skilled, unskilled, men, women, black, white, immigrant, and native—to be united in a single organization. Someday, they believed, they would be able to change American society and do away with what they thought was the cause of poverty: the "wage system." Under the wage system, one person owned the property—land or factory or mine—and paid wages to other people to work on it. The wages were determined by the owner, and the "wage-earners" were completely dependent on him. Almost every working person in those days knew from personal experience that owners paid as little as they could—regardless of the consequences for their employees. Though they needed the workers as a group, individual workers were not considered important. Any one of them could easily be replaced.

It seemed to the Knights that under the wage system, working people would always be treated badly. They wanted to replace the wage system with a cooperative system, under which the workers would own the property themselves, run it together, and share the profits.

The Knights knew that such a change would take a long time. Working people would have to be better educated. They would have to learn how to run a business, and they would have to accumulate enough money to buy property. To help the workers in the meantime, the Knights looked to the government. They believed that when enough workers were members of the Order, they could persuade the government to protect them by passing laws to regulate working conditions and wages.

Most workers' groups believed that strikes were the tactic workers should use. Since businesses slowed down or closed when workers called a strike and walked off their jobs, strikes were one way workers had of forcing their employers to deal with them. But the Knights did not believe in strikes. They did not think workers were strong enough to win them, and they disapproved of the violence that often accompanied them. The Knights were committed to changing the system, but they believed it could be done slowly and peacefully.

At the meeting, Mary took a seat in the back of the room and listened while the members talked about the ways they could make their organization grow and about how much better things would be when every worker was a Knight. They ended the meeting by rededicating themselves to the Knights' official slogan: "An injury to one is an injury to all."

When the meeting was over, Mary approached the chairman and said she would like to become a member. Giving her profession as "seamstress," Mary told him that her husband had been an iron molder and had worked for the union in Tennessee. But she had no family now, and she would like to help the Knights.

The chairman shook her hand, welcomed her, and told her about a meeting the group was holding on the weekend. Would she be able to join them?

Mary nodded and said she would be there. Then she quietly left the building.

❧ FIVE ❧

PANIC AND
THE GREAT UPHEAVAL

Mary had no experience as a public speaker. But in the weeks that followed the Great Chicago Fire, she found that she had a talent for it. She never raised her voice. If anything, it became deeper when she spoke and so intense that one friend said, "You could almost feel it, physically." It was melodic, with the echo of a lilt. People listened to Mary, and they were moved.

Mary had returned to her work as a seamstress after the fire, using one of the sewing machines the city provided to help the poor. But it was soon clear that her real work was the work she was doing for the Noble and Holy Order. Her involvement had come about naturally. The Knights held meetings every week, and Mary attended regularly. She joined the picnics and retreats they held on weekends. Before long, she helped to arrange meetings. Then she began traveling to different parts of Chicago, talking to workers who had not yet joined the Knights, and to those who didn't know the organization existed. She explained who the Knights were and what they believed in. She set up meetings and encouraged people to come. At the meetings she spoke, and urged them to join. In short, she was an organizer for the Knights.

As the weeks went by, Mary became a familiar figure to Chicago's poor, who were beginning the slow work of rebuilding their homes. (The city government had given each homeless family enough wood to build a one-room shanty.) The year 1871 passed. It had been a tragic one for the people of Chicago.

Two years later, 1873, was a tragic year for the entire nation. The cause this time was not something you could see or touch. It was a financial "panic"—as depressions were called in those days. It began on September 18, when America's leading brokerage house, Jay Cooke and Company, declared itself bankrupt and closed its doors.

The Cooke Company had invested millions of dollars in railroads, mines, and other industries across America. Banks as well as individuals had given their money to the brokerage house to invest for them. For a long time, businesses were booming, and investors earned enormous profits. But the boom had ended with the end of the Civil War, and the Cooke Company itself had begun to borrow huge sums of money. By 1873, it had borrowed more money than it would ever be able to repay.

The collapse of the Cooke Company set off a chain reaction which shook the country from coast to coast. Smaller banks and brokerage houses lost the funds they had entrusted to the Cooke Company. They closed. Private businesses lost the funds they had invested in the banks and brokerage houses. They closed. Factory owners could no longer sell all their products, so production slowed down. Mine owners could not sell all their ores and minerals to the factories, so mines closed. Across the nation, hundreds of thousands of people were thrown out of work.

Shantytowns sprang up on vacant lots, built by people who had been evicted from their homes when they could no longer pay the rent. Thousands of people wandered across the nation in search of work and food and shelter. In the winter, these "tramps" collected in cities, begging for food, sleeping in hallways and under bridges. By the spring, four million people were out of work. New York, Chicago, and San Francisco recorded many deaths due to starvation.

In hundreds of towns and cities, unemployed men and women marched, demonstrated, and begged for food—and work. Police and militia were called out to disperse them. In Tompkins Square in New York City, mounted police turned their clubs on a crowd of demonstrators and sent them running through the streets in terror. In Chicago, where Mary was living, 20,000 people gathered and marched together to the city hall. Their flag, bearing the chilling slogan, "BREAD OR BLOOD," fluttered in the icy wind.

Mary watched the scene sadly. She was still a newcomer to the labor movement, and she did not play a major role in any of the strikes and protests that flared up in and around Chicago. Nor did she take a position of leadership within the Knights of Labor. Nevertheless, relatively young, well educated, and a woman, she was an unusual figure in the circle of labor organizers in which she moved. The Knights had not yet begun to accept local groups or "Assemblies" of women workers. Though they accepted individual women on an equal basis with men, very few had joined, and none was an active organizer like Mary. Outspoken and straightforward, she was an exception wherever she went.

Thousands of people were made homeless by the panic. Like the men in the photo, they slept wherever they could.

In later years, Mary would encourage working women to join unions and stand up for their rights, and she would encourage women whose husbands were on strike to join the struggle. Women had not been granted the right to vote, but Mary did not think that mattered. "I have never had a vote," she said once, "and I have raised hell all over this country. You don't need a vote to raise hell. You need convictions and a voice." She had special scorn for people who said it was "unladylike" for women to be active. "A lady is the last thing on earth I want to be," she said, calling ladies "parlor parasites," created by the class of wealthy men to be decorative, entertaining—and unimportant.

Mary had not come into her own yet—she had no special following and no special message. But she was on her way to becoming the original and unflappable "mother" of America's working class.

Throughout the 1870s, the Depression deepened. No one, not even the Knights, seemed able to help the workers. Those who had managed to hold on to their jobs had to accept wage cuts so severe that they could barely pay for food and rent. Many workers wanted the Order to help them organize strikes and they wanted it to set up a "strike fund," a reserve of money for workers to use while they were on strike.

But the Knights held back, insisting that strikes could not be won and that workers who called them would only get hurt. From time to time, local Assemblies of Knights defied the leaders and called strikes on their own. Then the Order would step in—reluctantly—with advice, and sometimes with money.

Mary too began to wonder whether the Knights were correct in their attitudes. But she did not challenge the Order's leaders or organize workers on her own. Then, in 1877, a railroad strike began which was so momentous that many people called it a "revolution." It was just the sort of thing the Knights wanted to stay away from. But Mary plunged into the middle of it.

The strike, which came to be called "The Great Upheaval," began with a small group of workers in the little town of Martinsburg, fifty miles outside of Washington, D.C. Before it was over, millions of dollars worth of railroad property would be destroyed, hundreds of workers would be shot and killed, and federal soldiers would be sent to railroad towns across America.

The railroad industry was then America's most profitable business. Since the Civil War, 33,000 miles of track had been laid, opening up the country to settlers—and to businessmen and other people who had something to sell. But the Panic of 1873 put a stop to the construction of new lines, and some of the existing ones had to close down. Owners and stockholders on the lines which remained open could continue to earn their usual 10 percent profit only if they decreased the cost of operating their railroads. They did so by reducing the salaries of their employees. Wages were cut, and cut again. By 1876, salaries were 35 percent lower than they had been in 1873. Profits to stockholders, however, were the same as ever.

The railroad companies took further measures to keep profits up. Fares to passengers were raised often and without warning, a practice that angered the public. But with only one railroad serving any one area, the companies knew that the people could not take their business elsewhere.

The railroads fired thousands of workers and ordered those still employed to take out "double-headers"—twice the number of cars and twice the amount of work, at regular pay. Railroad owners stopped making repairs—for repairs cost money—and hundreds of workers were killed by corroded boilers which exploded and neglected trestles which collapsed. Workers protested and were ignored. Jay Gould, one of the mightiest railroad magnates, dismissed the poverty of his workers with a shrug. When someone suggested that the day might come when they would fight him, he was unruffled. "I can hire one half of the working class to kill the other half," he said.

In the spring of 1877, the Pennsylvania Railroad ordered its fourth wage cut. In the summer, the B & O Railroad did the same. The workers, already desperately poor, were told of the cut as they reported to the train yards for assignments. In Martinsburg, over 1,000 men rebelled. They refused to take the trains out unless the wage cut was canceled. In a further act of defiance, they vowed not to leave the yard or let any freight-carrying trains go through.

The mayor ordered the police to remove the strikers. But townspeople poured into the yard—families of the strikers as well as plain citizens who had heard the news and who themselves were angered by the rising fares. The people stood beside the trainmen and dared the police to arrest them all. A reporter for the Baltimore *Sun* noted especially the strikers' wives and mothers. "They look famished and wild," he wrote, "and declare for starvation rather than have their people work for the reduced wages."

The police, confronted by thousands of people—men, women, and children—pulled back, and the mayor dismissed them.

The next day, the state militia was ordered to the scene. But when, in a moment of confusion, gunshots were exchanged and a striker fell dead, discipline disintegrated and the troops could not be forced to take any further action. The commander wired the governor that he could not get the strikers out of the yard. Many of the militia stayed behind and joined the strikers and the townspeople.

The governor, under pressure from the railroad company which claimed that its property had been taken over by a mob—illegally and without warrant—asked President Rutherford Hayes to send in federal troops. "If the rights of the strikers had been ... violated instead of that of the railroad corporations," one newspaper article quietly stated, "Governor Matthews would have hesitated a long time before he would have thought it his duty to call on the President for aid."

The President was sympathetic with the company. In addition, although the strikers had carefully allowed mail-carrying trains to go through, President Hayes said he thought the United States mails were "endangered." Four hundred federal soldiers arrived in Martinsburg the next day. It was the first time federal soldiers had been sent to intervene in a workers' strike.

The federal troops protected the engineers, brakemen, and firemen they brought with them, and the first freight train pulled out. The townspeople and the strikers could not stop them. Most of the trains that left under federal escort got no more than a few miles out of town, however. Lying in ambush near bridges and on hillsides were farmers, miners, and other workers from the surrounding countryside. They fired at the trains as they approached and forced them to turn back.

As news of the rebellion in Martinsburg sped to towns and cities down the line, other railroad workers across the country joined in. Within three days, trainmen backed up by the people in their communities had taken over the train yards in towns and cities throughout the United States. In place after place, local troops called out to put down the strikers joined them instead. "Many of us have reason to know what long hours and low pay mean," said an officer of a New York regiment. "Any movement that aims at one or the other will have our sympathy and support. We may be militiamen, but we are workmen first." The most powerful industry in America was stopped cold.

Still, the railroad companies refused to discuss the wage cut which had caused the strike. They would not negotiate, insisting that the workers were just "lawbreaking rioters" who should be arrested and taken away. Tom Scott, president of the Pennsylvania Railroad, said he thought the workers should be given "a rifle diet for a few days and see how they like that kind of bread." And though the great majority of Americans sided with the railroad workers, the rich and powerful owners found friends among other wealthy Americans. In Plymouth Church in fashionable Brooklyn Heights, Henry Ward Beecher, the "rich man's pastor," laughed about the strikers with his prosperous congregation. "Is not a dollar a day enough to buy bread?" the Reverend asked. "Water costs nothing. . . . A family may live on good bread and water in the morning, water and bread at midday, and good water and bread at night."

In Pittsburgh, where the major railroad yard of the mammoth B & O Railroad was located, the events of Martinsburg were repeated. But this time the rebellion reached a climax. Mary was there when it happened.

Many organizers had volunteered to help the railroad workers, for the strike had begun spontaneously, without leadership, plans, or money to back up the strikers. Experienced people had stepped in to help with the nuts and bolts of the strike—raising money, collecting food, setting up distribution centers, keeping the people in the community informed about what was happening in the railroad yard. When Mary arrived in Pittsburgh, she joined other volunteers. She participated with great energy, marching on picket lines, collecting and distributing food, and trying—without success—to persuade a company representative to meet with a committee of workers. Her presence did not shape or change the course of events, but the strike made a deep impression on her. Though they might lose, the workers were standing up against a powerful industry. Never had the United States seen such an uprising. Mary had never before seen working people so united or so strong.

Mary was in the train yard when the announcement came that the mayor of Pittsburgh had called up the local militia. Half of those called did not report for duty, but Mary watched as the ones who did report arrived.

Would they use their weapons on the strikers? They would not. "The sympathy of the people, the sympathy of the troops, my own sympathy," an officer said later, "was with the strikers proper." Instead of dispersing the trainmen, the troops milled around and spoke to them. When noon came and food was distributed, the soldiers sat down to eat with the strikers.

The next day, the governor of Pennsylvania, realizing that local units of the state militia could not be relied upon, ordered troops to be sent from Philadelphia. But by the time the troops arrived, more than 6,000 people were massed on the tracks to prevent them from entering.

The troops were ordered to make their way through the crowd. Fixing their bayonets in place, they marched toward the people. Someone—witnesses said it was children—threw stones at them. The soldiers charged and some of them opened fire. Within seconds, twenty-six people were dead. A reporter from the New York *Herald* described the scene. "The sight presented after the soldiers ceased firing was sickening. . . . numbers of children were killed outright. Yellowside, the neighborhood of the scene of the conflict, was actually dotted with the dead and the dying . . . weeping women . . . were clinging to the bleeding corpses."

A grand jury which later investigated the shooting said it had been "wilfull [*sic*] and wanton killing . . . which can be called by no other name than murder."

The people on the tracks went wild. Shrieking and crying, they ran toward the soldiers who fled into the "roundhouse," a low structure at the end of the yard. Some of the soldiers dropped their weapons in their haste. Men and women in the crowd picked them up.

As word of the shooting spread through Pittsburgh, people rushed to the railroad yard. The crowd grew until it was almost 20,000 strong. People spilled over into the streets nearby and crowded onto the hill just beside the roundhouse. There the railroad company had freight cars full of oil, coke, and whiskey. They had been due to pass through Pittsburgh and had been stopped by the strike.

Cries of "Burn them! Burn the murderers out!" filled the air as the people on the hill set the cars on fire and pushed them toward the roundhouse. Soon flames were shooting and leaping against the walls.

Fire wagons arrived, but the angry mob kept them away. The flames rose higher and higher.

Finally, the doors of the roundhouse opened, and the soldiers came out. Racing to the woods on the other side of the yard, some of them tore off their shirts as they ran, to hide the fact that they

Philadelphia troops firing into the crowd in Pittsburgh, July 21, 1877.

were soldiers. Amid a shower of bricks and stones, they disappeared in the night.

Mary was in the crowd which stayed on the hillside watching the flames until the early hours of the morning. No one knew what would happen next. Sometime after the fire in the roundhouse died down, and the crowd went home, another fire was set. One hundred and five locomotives and seventy-nine buildings belonging to the railroad were destroyed, at a loss to the company of over 5 million dollars.

The next day, President Hayes sent federal troops to Pittsburgh. These men were neither friends nor neighbors of the Pittsburgh strikers. They were trained to obey their orders without question. They drove the people away, rounded up and arrested hundreds of strikers. The trains moved out once again. In the week that followed, federal troops were sent to city after city to clear the train yards. The Upheaval had begun on the fourteenth of July. It was over by the second of August.

Most of the workers returned to their jobs to find that nothing had changed. In a very few cases, the wage cut which had prompted the strike was canceled. But for the majority, the cut remained in effect, as did the long hours, the double-headers, and the dangerous conditions. Nevertheless, the workers had gotten the first real glimpse of their own strength. They began to understand how powerful they could be—when they were united. This understanding would send thousands into the ranks of the unions in the years to come. And it would send Mary back to Chicago, and to the Knights of Labor, troubled and impatient with the Order's attitude toward strikes.

The lesson was not lost on employers either. They saw the workers' potential power and determined to prevent them from uniting again. From this time on, spies, detectives, and guards were a regular part of company payrolls. The companies would keep their eyes on the state militia, too, and use their influence to get people they knew appointed to positions of authority. The battle lines were being drawn between employers and workers. It would be a cruel, uneven match.

The companies were well satisfied with the role the federal government had played. But working people—strikers and non-strikers alike—viewed it now with suspicion and bitterness. It had given the railroad companies a free hand and had stepped in only when the workers' despair boiled over and became rebellion. Then it intervened—to protect company property. Across the country, hundreds of workers had been shot by soldiers of their own government.

This attitude on the part of the government, its willingness to protect industry and its unwillingness to protect the people, would change in years to come. But in those days, America was just becoming a powerful nation, and industry was the key to its growth. The owners of industry had a great deal of influence on politicians. They could—and did—claim that the Great Upheaval, by disrupting the most basic industry of all, was a threat to the nation itself. So, the government felt justified in ending the strike by force.

Why hadn't the government stepped in earlier—to help the workers before conditions turned them into rebels? One reason was the American belief in "individualism"—the belief that each man could improve his own life, if only he was willing to work hard enough and long enough. The other was the American belief in "small government"—the belief that government should stay in the background, and interfere as little as possible with the way citizens lived. People believed, as Thomas Jefferson had written one hundred years earlier, that "that government is best which governs least."

These beliefs about the power of the individual and the role of the government had been born in a simpler time, before the rise of factories and industries. They did not entirely fit the complicated country America had become. But they remained, confusing the issues between workers and owners. Unions, for example, could be viewed as "unfair" and "un-American," since every individual was supposed to stand on his own. The government was not supposed to interfere in the conflicts between employers and employees, since citizens were supposed to be "free" to work out their own solutions. The fact that owners and workers did not face each other as "free and equal citizens" was not fully recognized. Very few people, in fact, had the wisdom to understand the many changes which industrialism had brought. Fewer still knew how to deal with them.

But to the people who had been involved in the Great Upheaval, one fact was clear: federal troops had served the railroad industry as if they were its own private army.

"Those early years," Mary wrote, "saw the beginning of America's industrial life. Hand in hand with the growth of factories and the expansion of railroads . . . came strikes. Came violence. Came the belief in the hearts and minds of the workers that legislatures but carry out the will of the industrialists."

✹ SIX ✹

HAYMARKET

When Mary returned to Chicago after the end of the Great Upheaval, she met an up-and-coming member of the Knights of Labor, Terence V. Powderly. A gentle, mild-mannered man, Powderly believed in the Knights completely. Mary no longer did, and the two spent many evenings discussing the Order's methods and assumptions, and the problems faced by America's workers.

To Mary's questions about the Order's refusal to call strikes, Powderly replied that not strikes but "gentle pressure" on the government would improve the lives of the workers. "Education and legislation," he said, were the tools the Knights must use. He was very upset by the violence of the Upheaval—and he used it to prove that strikes were futile and barbaric.

Mary didn't claim to know what the government might be like in the future. Perhaps a cooperative system would be created one day. But in the meantime, hundreds of thousands of people were

Terence V. Powderly.

living and dying in terrible poverty, and no one was helping them. If they had to help themselves, it seemed to her, they had to strike. For only by temporarily shutting down its business could they force a company to deal with them.

To Powderly's claim that strikes could not be won, Mary replied that they would have to be. If the workers weren't strong enough, shouldn't the leaders see to it that they became stronger? If they had no money to fall back on, shouldn't the leaders be out trying to raise it? If they had to face thugs and gunmen and soldiers to win justice, shouldn't their leaders stand before them, at their head?

Terence and Mary debated the problems time and again. They never came to an agreement, but they respected each other's honesty and devotion, and they became lifelong friends.

Mary may have traveled over the next few years, but there are no clear records of her comings and goings. Chicago became her "home base," however, and if she traveled, she always returned to it. Still officially a member of the Knights, Mary took odd jobs as a seamstress, and for a time may have managed a boarding house. But as the 1880s began, Chicago was, in her words, "a city filled with hunger and rags and despair." Unemployed men and women drifted silently into the city and out again searching for work. The Chicago *Tribune,* a newspaper which Mary noted bitterly was a "tool of the employers," satirically suggested that the farmers of Illinois treat the "tramps" that came pouring out of the city "as they did other pests, by putting strychnine in their food."

Another financial panic hit the country in 1882, just at the time that waves of poor immigrants began to arrive from Europe. They arrived at the rate of half a million a year for the rest of the 1880s. With so many people competing for a very limited number of jobs, employers were able to reduce wages even further and add even more hours to the work day.

As conditions for great masses of Americans grew worse and worse, radical groups and political parties sprang up in many cities. Mary attended the meetings of many of the groups in Chicago, which had become a center of radical activity. All of them had a certain appeal for her, as they did for the working people she wanted to help. Their leaders made exciting speeches and promised a "new and wonderful" future. But Mary soon realized that most of them never explained how this wonderful future would be brought about—or even what it would contain, except "justice and happiness" for "everyone." It seemed to her that they had no practical plans or programs at all.

The most controversial of the groups was the Anarchist party. It did not have many members, but its activities were widely reported in the press because they were so shocking. The anarchists believed that governments existed in order to protect the people who owned the land and the factories. Just look at America, they said, at the masses of ordinary people who are poverty-stricken and miserable. Then you will know that the government is not being run to protect them. The anarchists believed that someday they would be able to eliminate the government altogether and create a society in which there would be no laws at all, except those of cooperation and respect among all people. In the meantime, however, they urged working people to buy guns and other weapons for the day when they might have to defend themselves against the "armed hirelings" of the government—soldiers and police.

Some anarchists became deeply involved in the union movement in Chicago. Mary went to the meetings they held on the windy lakefront "to hear," she wrote, "what these bringers of a new order had to say." But although many of the leading anarchists seemed motivated by a sense of justice much like Mary's, she thought that on the whole they did more harm than good. Their talk of violence, she wrote, and the dramatic marches they held, headed by the black flag of anarchy and the red flag of revolution, "only served to make feelings more bitter ... to increase the employers' fears, to make the police more savage and the public less sympathetic to the real distress of the workers." She noted sadly that "the people asked only for bread, and a shortening of the long hours of toil. The agitators gave them visions. The police gave them clubs." And Chicago began to "seethe with unrest."

In a single month in 1885, there were strikes among the lake seamen, the dockworkers, and the streetcar operators. None of them was won. Mary witnessed it all and watched Chicago become more divided than ever. Now, she wrote, there were "two angry camps. The working people on one side—hungry, cold, jobless—and the employers on the other, knowing neither hunger nor cold."

The two sides finally clashed in a murderous encounter in Haymarket Square on the first of May, 1886. Eleven people were killed in the gunfight that took place there after a bomb exploded at a workers' rally.

The rally had been called in connection with the "Eight-Hour Movement," a drive of workers all over the country to shorten the work day to eight hours. In many industries, men and women worked fourteen and even sixteen hours a day. Ten and twelve hours were the average. Now, 400,000 workers across America planned to strike on the first of May if their employers did not grant them the eight-hour day.

Chicago was one of the most active centers of the Eight-Hour Movement. Mary was not a major figure in its planning, but she gave it her wholehearted support, speaking at meetings and collecting funds which would be needed if, as seemed likely, the strike was called. Rallies and meetings were held throughout the city, attended by thousands of working people. The Eight-Hour Song could be heard almost everywhere:

> *We want to feel the sunshine*
> *We want to smell the flowers*
> *We're sure that God has willed it*
> *And we mean to have eight hours.*

The stronger the movement grew, the more bitterly it was opposed by employers. Mary watched Chicago's businessmen grow "open and defiant in the expression of their fears and hatreds." Adding fuel to the old feeling that unions themselves were "un-American" was the fact that so many of the workers were immigrants. And when a number of well-known Chicago anarchists became leaders of the movement in that city, the movement itself was branded "anarchistic" and "traitorous." Guards and private police were hired and ordered to stand by. Workers were asking for a shorter work day; employers reacted as though they were planning a revolution.

Nevertheless, for a while it seemed as though the movement might succeed. Even before the strike deadline, 150,000 workers throughout the United States were granted an eight-hour day by their employers. And on the first of May, when the call to strike went out, workers responded so enthusiastically, and in such great numbers, that employers granted the shorter day to 40,000 more. By the second of May, the workers seemed on the verge of victory. An article in a workers' newspaper described the feeling: "It is an eight-hour boom and we are seeing victory after victory. The men are wild with joy."

Late in the afternoon of the third of May, strikers were picketing outside the giant McCormick Harvester Works on the south side of Chicago. The McCormick plant managers had hired "strikebreakers"—people who were willing to work for them in spite of the fact that a strike was going on. The strikers had set up a picket line. As police watched, they marched around the plant, carrying signs that said, "We are on strike for an eight-hour day." They called in to the strikebreakers, urging them to come out and join them. "Close the plant! Close the plant!" they chanted. "Come on out! Eight hours for everyone!"

When the work shift changed, the strikebreakers filed outside and some of them got into a fight with the pickets. The police opened fire. Four pickets were killed and two more were wounded.

A protest meeting was called by Chicago's labor unions for the following night in Haymarket Square, an open area bordered by warehouses and factories. Mary did not attend the meeting, but she knew the site well. A block away was the Des Plaines Street police station, "presided over," she wrote, by "Captain John Bonfield, a man without . . . sympathy, a most brutal believer in suppression as the method to settle industrial unrest."

About a thousand people attended the meeting. They heard the speakers—anarchists and other leaders in the Eight-Hour Movement—protest police brutality. One of them urged the people to

Attention Workingmen!

GREAT

MASS-MEETING

TO-NIGHT, at 7.30 o'clock,

AT THE

HAYMARKET, Randolph St., Bet. Desplaines and Halsted.

Good Speakers will be present to denounce the latest atrocious act of the police, the shooting of our fellow-workmen yesterday afternoon.

Workingmen Arm Yourselves and Appear in Full Force!

THE EXECUTIVE COMMITTEE.

Achtung, Arbeiter!

Große

Massen-Versammlung

Heute Abend, ½8 Uhr, auf dem

Heumarkt, Randolph-Straße, zwischen Desplaines- u. Halsted-Str.

☞ Gute Redner werden den neuesten Schurkenstreich der Polizei, indem sie gestern Nachmittag unsere Brüder erschoß, geißeln.

☞ Arbeiter, bewaffnet Euch und erscheint massenhaft!

Das Executiv-Comite.

An announcement of the meeting in Haymarket Square to protest the killing of strikers outside the McCormick Harvester plant. It is written in two languages.

buy weapons so that the next time police fired at workers, they would not be unarmed, as the strikers at the Harvester plant had been. Yet, upset as the speakers and the people were about the shootings, there were no disturbances. The mayor of Chicago came to the square and left, feeling assured that there was no danger of violence or rioting.

A newspaper engraving of the bombing at Haymarket Square.

The meeting was almost over—the last speaker was climbing onto the small wagon which served as a platform—when a cold rain started. People began to drift away, leaving a crowd of less than 300 in the square.

Suddenly, a contingent of almost 200 police officers appeared, surrounded the square, and told Samuel Fielden, the man speaking, to step down.

"But, officers, we are peaceable," he said, as he and another speaker began to climb down.

At that instant, there was a blinding red flash and a burst of noise. A bomb had been thrown near the line of police. Several officers and more than thirty bystanders fell to the ground.

The police turned and fired into the crowd. People began to scream and run from the square. Those who had weapons—many people carried guns and knives in those days—shot back at the charging police. Others picked up bricks and rocks and hurled them as they fled. In all, seven policemen and ten workers were killed.

The next day, headlines across the country described the "Haymarket Riot," and the "bloodthirsty savages" who had attacked the police. The city of Chicago declared a state of emergency. All meetings were declared "dangerous" and were broken up by squads of police who honeycombed working-class neighborhoods. "Make the raids first and look up the law afterwards," said Illinois' chief attorney.

In newspapers in Chicago and throughout the country, the anarchists as a group were blamed, even though there was no proof that any one of them had planned the bombing, much less thrown the bomb. "There are no good anarchists except dead anarchists," said the St. Louis *Democrat.*

With this hateful condemnation of the anarchists went a condemnation of the entire Eight-Hour Movement, for now the two were thought of as one. "Anyone who favors an eight-hour day is a scurrilous traitor," said the Chicago *Tribune*. Throughout the country, workers' meetings were prohibited and leaders of the Eight-Hour Movement arrested. Curfews were imposed. The drive for a shorter work day was stamped out.

"The bomb was a godsend to the enemies of the labor movement," wrote John Swinton, a noted labor historian of the period. "The workers' cry for justice was drowned in the shriek for revenge," wrote Mary.

Within the week, eight well-known Chicago anarchists were arrested for the bombing. In a trial that was later proved to be one of the most unfair in American history, all eight were convicted. Seven were sentenced to death by hanging.

The trade unions tried to rally public opinion in support of the condemned men, but the atmosphere was too frenzied. The Knights of Labor offered no aid. Though they had supported the Eight-Hour Movement, they had never been happy with the strike plan, and when the pickets were killed at the McCormick plant, they felt that they had been right to stay out of it. After the Haymarket bombing, they refused to work for the condemned men, claiming it was more important to keep the Order free from any association with anarchists and bombs. "Better that seven times seven men hang," wrote Terence Powderly, who had become the leader of the Knights, "than to hang the millstone of odium around the standard of the Order in affiliating in any way with this element of destruction." He believed that he was acting only "to save the organization I have worked so hard to build." But Mary found his attitude a betrayal of the people.

Controversy about the trial and the men condemned to death raged throughout the summer. In a last-minute decision, the sentences of two of the men were commuted to life imprisonment. The other five were to be executed. One of them escaped the gallows by committing suicide in his cell. In November, the remaining four, Albert Parsons, August Spies, Adolph Fischer, and George Engle, were hung.

Thousands of people, Mary wrote, "marched behind the black hearses, not because they were anarchists, but they felt that these men, whatever their theories, were martyrs to the workers' struggle." The procession wound through "miles and miles of streets densely packed with silent people." The Knights maintained their distance. The funeral, held at Waldheim Cemetery, was attended by 25,000 people. Mary was one of them. "The dead were buried," she wrote, "but with them was not buried their cause. The struggle for an eight-hour day, for more human conditions and relations between man and man lived on and still lives on."

Seven years later, John Peter Altgeld was elected governor of Illinois. He spent a year studying the records of the trial, sifting through the evidence that had been used to convict the men. His study convinced him that they had all been entirely innocent. He ordered the three men still in prison released, and he wrote a detailed explanation of his action.

As Mary and many other people had believed at the time, the men convicted of the Haymarket bombing had been framed. Police officials, the governor now revealed, had jailed, threatened, and bribed witnesses and had told them what to say.

Governor Altgeld's statement was bitterly denounced by industrialists, businessmen, law enforcement agencies—and thousands of people who had believed the newspaper reports at the time and had added their voices to the cry for blood. Altgeld's action ended his political career. He was never elected to public office again.

Governor Altgeld, Mary wrote years later, "committed political suicide by his brave action, but he is remembered by all those who love truth and those who have the courage to confess it."

After the Haymarket Affair, Mary left Chicago to travel on her own. Although she and Terence Powderly remained lifelong friends, she was no longer officially connected with the Knights. Its reluctance to meet problems "head on" had been disturbing to her for some time. Its cold response to the Haymarket Affair persuaded her to leave it altogether. She was not sure what she would do, or where she would go, but she knew she could not stand on the sidelines any longer.

᠅ SEVEN ᠅

FIRST STEPS

Mary's whereabouts for several years after the Haymarket Affair are hard to trace. She had no permanent address, and since even in her autobiography these years are unaccounted for, there is no way of knowing exactly what she did or how she lived. This lack of information made it possible for gossip-mongers to slander her later on. But after 1890, Mary's name begins to appear in accounts of strikes in several different parts of the country. When it does, she is called "Mother" Jones.

In 1891, Mary was in Norton, Virginia, helping coal miners who had gone on strike. There were many strikes in the coal fields during the 1890s. Most of them involved a new union, the United Mine Workers of America. It had been founded in the last months of 1889, and its organizers had set out to establish local branches in Illinois, Pennsylvania, Virginia, and West Virginia.

Representatives had been working in Norton for months before

Mary's arrival. When a local branch of the union was finally established, the Dietz Company, which owned the mines, fired the workers who had joined it. At this, the union called a strike. Mary may have heard about it from friends in the Knights of Labor. The miners' union had been part of the Knights at one time. In any case, when she learned of the strike, she decided to go to Norton to help. This was Mary's first coal strike, and though she did not know exactly what she would find, she knew that the situation would be difficult.

Mining, in Mary's words, was "cruel work." The men labored twelve or fourteen hours a day, six days a week, in dark pits deep underneath the ground. Often they had to crawl through damp underground passages to cramped "rooms"—less than three feet high—in which they worked. There, stooped and bent, they picked and shoveled tons of coal and loaded it by hand onto wagons and carts which were pulled out of the mine by donkeys or, if the passageway was too small, by dogs. Cave-ins were common. No one knew when a roof might collapse, crushing the miners' backs or legs, or burying them alive. Almost as common were explosions, for the slightest spark might ignite if enough methane gas, released when the coal was dug, was in the air.

Most coal mines were far from established towns and cities, so the miners lived in settlements—consisting of houses, a school, a church, a store—built by the company on company land near the mines. Tucked away in the mountains, these settlements were called "company towns."

Miners could not hold meetings, or have guests, or read books of which the company did not approve. The company hired the teacher and controlled what was taught in the schools. It hired the pastor, the doctor, and the storekeeper, and determined the prices

Miners with the dogs who pulled their coal-laden carts through narrow passageways in the mines.

charged at the company stores. These stores were called "pluck me" stores by the miners because they charged higher prices than free stores in free towns. The miners had to trade there, because their wages were given to them in the form of paper certificates called "scrip," rather than cash, and scrip was not accepted by the merchants at free stores.

Some miners quit their jobs if they could, and went to live somewhere else. But most of them were too poor to save any

money, certainly not as much as they would need to travel to another state and find another job. In fact, salaries were so low that many families ran out of money before payday. The company stores would encourage them to make purchases on credit—the amount to be deducted from future wages. So, by the time payday came, they owed money to the company.

The male children, raised and educated in the company towns, followed their fathers into the mines at an early age. The girls followed their mothers into the textile mills, or hard labor at home.

Organizing such people under these conditions was treacherous. Mary, in spite of her lack of experience, handled herself with great skill and confidence. It was true that as a woman, and an old woman at that (she was sixty-one years old in 1891), she could sometimes get away with things that male organizers could not. Company guards and local police often did not know what to make of her, and they treated her with caution. She could taunt a mine guard to "shoot an old woman if he dared." She could on occasion defy a police officer's order and be let off with only a reprimand. Other organizers were sometimes waylaid and beaten if they ventured out alone or after dark. Mary was not. But even so, it took courage for her to handle the situation she found when she arrived at the train station in Norton.

Company agents routinely checked the station, on the lookout for union organizers. Mary was spotted as a unionist and told to get back on the train and leave town. "The supervisor doesn't want to see your kind around these parts," the agent told her. "If he sees you, he'll blow your brains out."

"Tell the supervisor I am not coming to see him," Mary replied coolly. "I am coming to see the miners."

Mary joined the United Mine Workers organizers, even though she was not an official of the union. They were living in tents pitched on public land, for the hotel in town, under pressure from the Dietz Company, would not rent rooms to them. The organizers needed help badly, and volunteers were welcome. Mary was not well known at this time, although she may have met some of the men in Pittsburgh during the Great Upheaval. But she was serious about the job at hand, she knew a good deal about unions, and she was willing to work.

The organizers explained that they were trying to persuade all—or almost all—the miners to join the strike. Then the mines would close, and the company would have to deal with them. Mary could help by holding meetings and explaining to the miners that although they had no power as individuals, as a group—as a union—they did. For many miners, just seeing an organizer stand up to the company was an inspiration.

The day after she arrived, Mary set out to find a place in which to hold a meeting. She knew that if she so much as stepped on

This early photograph of Mary may have been taken near Norton, Virginia, where she went, alone, to help the strikers.

company land she would be arrested for trespassing. She tried at first to find a room to rent, but no one would rent to her. Like the hotel keeper, they had all been threatened by the company.

Mary held her meeting outside, on the public highway. After the meeting, she was arrested anyway, because the man with whom she was walking—another organizer, named Dud Hado—was carrying a gun.

Mary and Hado were taken to the local courthouse, where it was admitted that there were no charges against her. Hado was fined twenty-five dollars. Mary paid the fine for him and was later told that the local officials had counted on her to appeal the case. "Then they were going to lock you both up," her informant said, "and burn you in the coke ovens at night and say you had been turned loose in the morning and that they didn't know where you had gone."

Whether they really would have done this, Mary did not claim to know. But the struggles she had seen—from the Great Upheaval to the Eight-Hour Movement—were leading her to one cruel conclusion. "I do not know whether they would have carried out their plan to burn us," she wrote years later, "but I do know that there are no limits to which the powers of privilege will not go to keep the workers in slavery."

The strike at Norton in 1891 was lost. The miners who had been its leaders were fired, and the rest returned to work. The union was not able to establish a local branch in that year or for many years to come. But it would return, and when it did, Mary would be there. She was drawn to the miners more than to any other group of workers. The most savage conflicts in all of labor history would be waged among the coal miners, and Mary was always with them. She came to call the miners her "boys," and they trusted her and called upon her as they did no other outsider.

Three years after Norton, Mary saw her first massive coal strike when she joined 8,000 UMW workers who had gone out to protest a wage cut in the mines near Birmingham, Alabama. The National Guard had been called out. Soldiers were stationed on streetcorners and along the roads leading into the city. Picket lines were not allowed, and speeches of almost every kind were prohibited. "I was forbidden to hold meetings," Mary wrote, "forbidden to leave town without a permit." As in Norton, Mary was only one of many organizers working to help the miners, but she displayed a resourcefulness that would soon become her trademark. Once, when she was determined to speak to a group of miners in an area she knew would be closed to her, she used her age and sex—and her knowledge of the soldiers—to her advantage. "I slipped through the ranks without their knowing who I was," she wrote, "just an old woman going to a missionary meeting to knit mittens for the heathen of Africa."

The strike was three months old when it was announced that Eugene Debs, the man who had created the new American Railway Union for railroad workers, was coming to town. Debs's union had just been defeated in a nationwide strike, and Debs himself had just been released from jail. He had served six months for disobeying a court order that prohibited him from giving speeches during the strike. His courage and compassion had made him one of the best-loved people in the country. Now he was coming to rally the Birmingham members of his union and to encourage the striking miners.

At the Birmingham headquarters of the American Railway Union, Mary joined the Committee on Reception preparing for Debs's arrival. They rented an opera house for the speech Debs

Eugene Debs.

was to give, and they wrote advertisements and distributed them. They knew that the meeting would be very well attended.

Debs was scheduled to arrive on a Sunday afternoon, and to speak that evening. Just before his train was due, city officials announced that the meeting would not be allowed to take place. It would "threaten the peace." As an extra precaution, the owner of the opera house was notified that he would not be allowed to open the doors of his building.

When Mary heard of the prohibition, she contacted other UMW organizers and asked them to go to the nearby mining towns of Bessemer and Pratt, round up as many miners as they could, and bring them to the train station. Then she went to ARU headquarters, where a crowd had gathered. She suggested that they all go to the depot together to meet Debs's train.

The chairman of the Committee on Reception, who, Mary wrote, "didn't have much fighting blood in him," said he thought that only the members of the committee should go.

"I move that we all form a committee on reception," Mary said.

The crowd cheered and they all walked together to the station. Hundreds of miners from Bessemer and Pratt had already arrived, and the crowd was overwhelming.

When the train pulled in, the people "did not wait for the gates to open but jumped over the railing. They put Debs on their shoulders and marched out of the station . . . through the streets, past the railway office." Mary herself marched at the front of the procession. Debs later described the incident. Mary had gotten the workers together, he said admiringly, and "stood at their head as they fronted the enemy."

Mary noted with great satisfaction that "the chief of police had a change of heart." The opera house was opened to Debs, and the speech was given as scheduled. "That night the crowd heard a real sermon," Mary wrote, "by a preacher whose message was one of human brotherhood."

The miners of Birmingham held out for five months, but in the end the strike was broken and they returned to work. The other organizers left the city soon after, but Mary stayed behind. During the strike she had heard terrible stories of little children working in the textile mills around Birmingham. "I concluded the boys were overdrawing the picture," she wrote, "and I decided to find out for myself if what they said was true."

On her own, Mary traveled to the textile towns, going first to Cottondale, a sleepy town thirty miles outside of Birmingham. She went directly to the factory and applied for a job. The manager said that he would hire her only if she had a family that would also work in the mill. Did Mary have any children?

"Six," she answered, adding that she would move them all to Cottondale as soon as she found work for them. The manager was delighted and hired her on the spot. The next morning, she reported for work.

"And there," she said, "I saw the children."

Little girls and boys, barefooted, were walking up and down between the rows of spindles. "Tiny babies of six years old with faces of sixty did an eight-hour shift for ten cents a day," Mary learned. If they fell asleep, cold water was splashed on their faces. All day long they worked, while "the voice of the manager yelled above the ceaseless racket and whir of the machines."

The day shift began at five-thirty in the morning. From the entrance to the factory, Mary watched the long lines of "little gray children" come out of the fresh dawn into the noisy, lint-filled rooms.

At the lunch break, the children would fall asleep over their benches, or they would lie down on the bare floor. "Sleep was their recreation, their release," Mary said, "as play is to the free child."

When the work day was over, it was dark outside. Sometimes the younger children were afraid to go home. They would sleep on the floor till sunrise. When she could, Mary took the children home herself.

After two weeks, when her "family" still did not arrive, Mary sensed that the manager was growing suspicious. She quit, claiming that her husband was ill and could not make the trip. Then she moved on to Tuscaloosa where she got a job in a rope factory. This factory, too, was run almost entirely by children. They crawled under the machinery, oiling and cleaning. Accidents were common. She saw children whose hands had been crushed, others whose fingers had been snapped off.

Mary visited other towns in Georgia, South Carolina, and Alabama. In Selma, she worked in a mill and boarded with a woman whose eleven-year-old daughter, Maggie, worked in the mill too.

One Sunday a group of the girl's friends came to call for her. Maggie was still sleeping. When her mother went in to wake her, Mary overheard Maggie say that she was "tired enough to sleep forever."

The next day, Maggie went to the mill as usual. That afternoon, she was brought home dead. Her hair had been caught in the machinery, and her scalp had been torn off.

At last, exhausted by what she had seen, Mary left the South. "It seemed to me," she wrote years later, "that I could not look at those silent figures any longer. It seemed I must go North, to the grim coal fields, or to the Rocky Mountain camps, where the labor fight was at least being fought by grown men."

WITH THE MINERS IN WEST VIRGINIA

In 1897, a conference was held in Wheeling, West Virginia. The president of the United Mine Workers of America, John Ratchford, was there. So were Eugene Debs, John Sovereign, new leader of the Knights of Labor, and Samuel Gompers, president of the up-and-coming American Federation of Labor. And so was Mary Jones. The conference was called to discuss West Virginia, the state which contained the richest coal mines in the country, and the poorest workers. The United Mine Workers had begun an organizing drive early in the year. The drive turned into a strike when the coal companies fired all the workers who had joined the union. But now the strike and the drive were both floundering.

Mary's ability to rally people, her courage and her resourcefulness were recognized by President Ratchford when he invited her to attend the conference. He asked her to be an official organizer for the UMW, on salary, and authorized her to form local branches.

Mary went with a group of other UMW workers on a tour of the northern part of West Virginia. They, like the organizers who had gone before, realized that the union could not cope with the opposition it faced. The companies had hired armed guards on a massive scale. Strikers and organizers were beaten—dozens were hospitalized—as state and village police, as well as local judges, looked the other way. Many of them openly sided with the mining companies. Police officers arrested organizers on sight and charged them with "disturbing the peace." Strikers were arrested and charged with "loitering." Judges issued orders forbidding unionists to give speeches.

The strike did not even cause work in the mines to slow down, because the companies brought in strikebreakers, poor immigrants and blacks from distant cities who were not told about the strike when they were hired. They arrived on special trains and were escorted to the mines by armed guards. The strikers were not allowed anywhere near them. The companies also gave wage increases to miners who demonstrated their "loyalty" by pledging never to join the union, and bonuses to those who brought in the names of fellow workers who did. The wage hikes would be canceled as soon as the union was beaten. But even if the increases had remained, the companies would have considered it a fair trade. The union was a threat to their power, and they were willing to pay to.keep it out.

In late September, less than three months after the strike was begun, it ended and the UMW withdrew from West Virginia. Mary was asked to help with a drive being waged in the Pennsylvania coal fields. There, geography was kinder to the miners. They were not so cut off from the rest of the world, and the companies were not so powerful as they were in West Virginia.

Mary worked in the northern district. She traveled to camps and went into the mines, rallying the men and urging them to join the union. "Sometimes it was 12 or 1 o'clock when I would get home," she wrote later. "Sometimes it was several degrees below zero. The winds whistled down the mountains and drove the sleet and snow in our faces. My hands and feet were often numb. . . . I slept in a room that never had a fire in it and I often woke up in the morning to find snow covering the outside covers of the bed."

One fifteen-year-old miner, John Brophy, who later became an important leader in his own right, described how Mary operated. "She came into the mine one day and talked to us. . . . How she got in I don't know; probably just walked in and defied anyone to stop her . . . She would take a drink with the boys and spoke their idiom, including some pretty rough language when talking about the bosses. This might have been considered a little fast in ordinary women, but the miners . . . respected her. They might think her a little queer—it *was* an odd kind of work for a woman in those days—but they knew she was a good soul. She had a lively sense of humor—she could tell wonderful stories, usually at the expense of some boss, for she couldn't resist the temptation to agitate, even in a joke."

When a strike was called, Mary organized the women—wives and mothers of the strikers—to prevent strikebreakers from getting to the mines. She formed a group called the "mop and broom brigade," and it worked spectacularly. Mary chose as a leader a woman who, she later wrote, "had a most picturesque appearance." She had "a little red fringed shawl over her wild red

Children and men work alongside one another sorting coal.

hair. Her face was red and her eyes were mad. I looked at her and felt that she could raise a rumpus."

Mary sent the women, armed with pots, pans, brooms, and mops, to the mouth of the mine where strikebreakers were expected. When they came, on mule-drawn wagons, the women hollered, beat their dishpans, waved their mops about—and started

96

the mules stampeding down the mountain. "An army of strong mining women makes a wonderfully spectacular picture," she later told a congressional committee.

Mary went on to organize marches of miners and women throughout the district. The marches were a show of strength to the coal companies and helped to encourage thousands of miners to come out for the union. Mary's reputation among the people grew, although newspapers began to refer to her as "the Chicago virago" who was "out among the miners, urging disorder in a language that made the women hysterical and got the men to marching at daybreak." *The New York Times* wrote that "the presence of this woman is generally reprobated." And although John Mitchell, newly elected president of the UMW, publicly praised her work, he worried about the danger of conflicts with deputies.

Nevertheless, the UMW won important successes in the coal fields of northern Pennsylvania in the last years of the nineteenth century. When the drive began, 8,000 miners belonged to the UMW. When it was over, the union had 100,000 members there. The strike was won—the miners received a 10 percent wage increase, and Mary had begun to show what she could do.

"This is the time of Mother Jones," declared an article in *The Appeal to Reason,* a workers' publication. "Her appearance is a signal for those who grow rich by grinding the faces of the poor to 'go slow,' and if they disregard the warning so much the worse for them and the better for organized labor."

Shortly after the settlement of the strike in northern Pennsylvania, the UMW began a new drive in West Virginia. Organizers were sent to the coal fields in both the northern and the southern parts of the state. John Mitchell asked Mary to take charge of activities in the South.

In this drive, Mary came into her own. Her energy and spirit drew the praises of everyone who saw her. "Our meetings were very tame indeed," wrote an organizer who had been in West Virginia for several weeks before Mary arrived, "until we were blessed with the presence of a new force. This new force is just what is needed. Mother Jones is attracting great attention and her meetings every night are increasing the enthusiasm for the union."

It was tough, demanding work, as hard on the body as it was at times on the spirit. Mary stayed with miners' families when she was up in the mountains. She ate what they ate and shared sleeping quarters with the children. She met her traveling and living expenses from the money paid her by the union. UMW records for the year 1900 state that "Mrs. Mary Jones" was paid a total of $494.81.

Often, even if Mary had the money, she would not order a meal that a miner could not afford. She would have felt, she wrote, that she was "filling her stomach at the expense of the wretches." And she expected her fellow-organizers to feel the same way. Many of them complained of her criticisms, and even those who loved and admired her found them hard to take. "Each of us has put forth every effort to avoid Mother's ire," wrote Fred Mooney, who worked with Mary in West Virginia and became one of her lifelong friends.

Making her way into a new area, Mary would visit the places where miners gathered—tavern, field, or crossroad store. She would introduce herself, talk to them about the union, and, if they could read, give them union literature. When she thought there was enough interest, she would call a meeting. They were held at night, in the woods, away from company property and hopefully out of the sight of company spies.

She may have been something of a mystery to the miners, a sweet-faced old woman taking on their cause at the risk of her own safety. But she got through to them. Her style was colorful and flamboyant. She would shout, stamp her foot, and gesture with her hands. She appealed to them not as a "professional," not even as an equal, but as a mother.

Sometimes she scolded them. "If you would just use your brains instead of your mouths, but you do not," she said to one group of miners. "The workingman has not kept pace," she said to another group. "They do not think. . . . they just go on like dumb animals."

Sometimes she shamed them, appealing to their pride, their sense of themselves as men. "I have been in jail more than once," she said at one meeting, "and I expect to go again. If you are too cowardly to fight, I will fight. You ought to be ashamed of yourselves, actually to the Lord you ought, just to see one old woman who is not afraid of all the bloodhounds."

Sometimes she accused them, in harsh, angry words, of being to blame for their problems. "Damn you!" she called out to a crowd in Williamson, West Virginia, "you are not fit to live! Of every ton of coal you mined, so much was taken out to hire professional murderers to keep you in subjection. You paid for it! You stood there like a lot of cowards . . . and you let yourself be robbed by the mine owners—and then you go about shaking your rotten heads. Not a thing inside!" The miners stood to applaud her. Whether she scolded them, shamed or blamed them, they knew that she meant to get them "up off their knees," as she told them time and again. She wanted them to face their employers with dignity and pride. "None of these fellows are better than you," she cried. "They are only flesh and blood—that is the truth!"

When Mary called a meeting, they came. When she cried out, "Join the union, boys!" they joined.

As a woman—as a mother—Mary fit into a pattern that was familiar and comfortable to the miners, for women were central figures in their families. With the men away in the mines for almost all their waking hours, with countless fathers, husbands, and sons killed and crippled on the job, it was the women who held things together and kept the families going. Though husbands and wives alike were quick to say that the man was the head of the house—in accordance with the tradition—in fact it was the wives and mothers who made decisions, gave advice, guided and governed the family. Mary might have been unique as a "woman organizer," but as a woman who cared about the miners, who called their problems her own, who argued with them, scolded them, and urged them to stand up for themselves "like men," she fit into a pattern already established by the miners' wives and mothers.

A union rally in West Virginia. The crowd is listening to Mother Jones, the figure on the speaker's platform.

Sometimes, too, Mary spoke to the men in the religious language they were used to. "The labor movement was not created by man," she said to one group in West Virginia. "The labor movement, my friends, was a command from God Almighty. He commanded the prophet to redeem the Israelites that were in bondage . . . he organized the men into a union . . . led them out of the land of bondage and robbery and plunder into the land of freedom."

Although Mary often appealed to the miners in terms of their religious beliefs, she had nothing but contempt for the churches and the ministers themselves. "Them fellows," she said once, "are owned body and soul by the ruling class. . . . Do you find a minister preaching against the guards? They will preach about Jesus, but not about the guards." The mine owners, she said, cheat, rob, and starve their workers, "and then they give to Jesus on Sunday. . . . Jesus never sees it and never heard of it!" she cried. "I wish I was God Almighty! I would throw down something some night from heaven and get rid of the whole blood-sucking bunch."

Mary urged the miners not to be "hoodwinked" by an institution which did not care about them. The group they should belong to was the union, not the church. "No church in the country would get up a crowd like this," she said at one meeting, "because we are doing God's holy work. . . . All the churches here and in heaven couldn't put the fear of God into the robbers, but our determination has made them tremble."

Many journalists tried to explain "the phenomenon of Mother Jones." They wrote about her "firm, hearty handshake," her "keen eyes and vigorous manner," and her "warm, strong personality." One reporter said that when she spoke about the way things might be in the future, her face glowed. Another said that "her earnestness would carry conviction to a steel magnet itself." She made people feel, he said, "as though she and they together could do anything."

The best glimpse into Mary and the work she was doing comes from a reporter for the Boston *Herald*. He saw Mary speak in West Virginia in the spring of 1901. He was so moved that he took down almost every word.

About 700 people had gathered in a field outside a mining camp. It was dusk, and one of the miners stood near her, holding a torch. Mary climbed onto a boulder and looked out at the men and their families.

"Has anyone ever told you, my children," she said, "about the lives you are living here, so that you may understand how it is you pass your days on earth? Have you told each other about it and thought it over among yourselves, so that you might imagine a brighter day and begin to bring it to pass? If no one has done so, I will do it for you today. Let us consider this together, for I am one of you, and I know what it is to suffer."

So the old lady, standing very quietly, in her deep, far-reaching voice, painted a picture of the life of a miner from his young boyhood to his old age. It was a vivid picture. She talked of the first introduction a boy had to those dismal caves under the earth, dripping with moisture, often so low that he must crawl into the coal veins, must lie on his back to work. She told how miners stood bent over until the back ached too much to straighten, or in sulphur water that ate through the shoes and made sores on the flesh; how their hands became cracked and their nails broken off in the quick;

how the bit of bacon and beans in the dinner pail failed to stop the craving of their empty stomachs, and the thought of the barefoot children at home and the sick mother was all too dreary to make the home-going a cheerful one. . . .

"You pity yourselves," she said, "but you do not pity your brothers, or you would stand together to help one another." And then in an impassioned vein she called upon them to awaken their minds so that they might live another life. As she ceased speaking, men and women looked at each other with shamed faces, for almost everyone had been weeping.

Under Mary's leadership, in the fall and winter of 1901–1902, the union began to make progress in the southern part of West Virginia. In the Kanawha Valley, a key area and the place where Mary put in the most time and energy, two strong locals were organized and two more were in the offing. With the arrival of spring, organizers throughout the state began to prepare for a statewide strike to begin in June. By April, Mary could send this cheerful report to union headquarters: "I am having glorious meetings. The boys are responding to the high call, and I think we will give you the Kanawha River organized by the first of May."

No such good reports were coming in from the north, however. Unlike the south, where over a dozen independent companies were involved in separate campaigns to stop the union, in the north only four companies owned all the mines. They had joined together and exercised iron-fisted control over the entire territory. The union had made hardly any progress there. As the strike date grew closer, President Mitchell told Mary that he would like to switch her from the southern to the northern coal fields.

"The coal operators there [in the north] have evidently scared our boys," he wrote to Mary, "and of course with good reason, as they have brutally beaten some of them. I dislike to ask you always to take the dangerous fields, but I know that you are willing."

Mary was to assume a position second in command to Thomas Haggerty, who had been in the north for some months. But shortly after Mary's arrival—and just before the strike began— Haggerty was arrested. Mary took over the entire field.

On the seventh of June, the strike began. Sixteen thousand workers throughout West Virginia, out of a total of almost 25,000 in the state, left the mines. They moved out of their company-owned houses and lived in tents on the hillsides.

Almost immediately, the companies began their counter-campaign to end the strike. Violence intensified as the number of company guards in the area increased. Shootings and beatings were everyday occurrences. Two union officers were almost killed one night on their way to the miners' camps. The train on which they were riding had stopped in the middle of a narrow trestle which spanned a deep canyon. Railroad guards walked through the passenger car and told the other passengers, one by one, to come with them to the car in front. The union officers were told to keep their seats, that after a minor adjustment was made they would soon be on their way again. Suddenly, the car just ahead was detached from the car in which the unionists sat, and the train pulled on, leaving them behind. In the pitch-black night, they had to crawl over the trestle on their hands and knees to the safety of the other side.

On another occasion, Mary had arranged to meet two fellow organizers near a bridge on the outskirts of the town where they were to hold a meeting. She got to the meeting place early and

A UMW tent colony, where miners lived while they were on strike.

was waiting alone in the dark, when one of the men came scream-
ing across the bridge. He yelled that company guards had jumped
the other man, Joe Battley, and were beating him to death.

Just at that moment, Mary heard an interurban trolley, a small
train commonly used in those days between towns and villages, in
the distance. She knew it would stop at the bridge—and that gave
her an idea.

"I ran toward the bridge," she wrote, "shouting 'Joe! Joe! The
boys are coming! The whole bunch of them! The car is almost
here! Hold on!' "

The trolley could be heard clearly now and the guards ran—as
Mary had intended them to do, leaving Joe alone on the bridge,
"the blood pouring out of him." Mary tore her petticoat into
strips, bandaged the man's head, and then she and the other organizer carried him aboard the interurban trolley. It had indeed
stopped at the bridge, although it was quite empty, except for the
tired, indifferent driver.

But as bad as violence and the threats of violence were,
the "injunctions"—legal orders forbidding people from making
speeches or holding meetings—were even more effective in block-
ing the union's efforts to reach the miners and keep the strike
going. Injunctions were issued by local judges—at the request of
the coal companies—usually on the grounds that the planned
meeting or speech would be "disruptive of the peace." "In West
Virginia," Mary said, "you can't step on a piece of ground without
you step on an injunction."

Mary knew that anyone who defied an injunction was likely to
be arrested and jailed, and thus cut off from the workers. But if
she obeyed the orders not to speak or hold meetings, she would be

cut off from them anyway. She chose to defy them. Let the authorities silence her if they could. She would not silence herself.

On the eleventh of July, just after concluding a speech at a strikers' colony, Mary was served with a writ forbidding all future meetings and demonstrations. But she defied it, and the next week, as she was speaking to another small group, she saw marshals move through the audience. Then they came to the speaker's platform and called Mary down.

"Good-bye, boys," she said, while the marshals stood waiting. "I'm under arrest. I may have to go to jail. I may not see you for a long time." Then she added, "Keep up this fight. Don't surrender. Pay no attention to the injunction machine at Parkersburg. The federal judge is a scab anyhow. While you starve, he plays golf. While you serve humanity, he serves injunctions for the money powers."

Mary was taken to the railroad station and placed on the train to Parkersburg, the county seat, along with eleven other organizers. On the train, she attempted—half-jokingly and half-seriously—to "instruct" the police officers guarding her with "a proper understanding of unionism." But she was in earnest a few hours later when she told a reporter that the judge who had issued the injunction was in cahoots with the mining companies. She also said that others would take her place in the field, and she pledged that the work would continue.

In fact, the strike was going badly. Armed guards, evictions, and blacklists were accomplishing what the mine companies intended them to: they were keeping the miners away from the union. And the injunctions were keeping the organizers away from the miners.

At the trial in Parkersburg, held on July 24, the judge made no attempt to hide the fact that he sided with the companies. He said that union organizers were "vampires that live and fatten on the honest labor of coal miners." They were "busybodies," he continued, "who create dissatisfaction." As if that were not bad enough, he had some additional thoughts for Mary.

Admitting that she seemed to be an "intelligent woman," he said she had not behaved like a "good woman." She had "strayed from the lines and paths which the Allwise Being intended her sex to pursue." If Mary wished to help "mankind in distress," the judge advised, she should devote herself to charity work, for that would be in keeping "with the true sphere of womanhood."

Mary responded by calling the judge a scab—which caused a furor among the spectators in the courtroom. But what she said next won applause. Speaking in her deep, earnest way, she said that she and His Honor were both old and that she hoped they could become good friends and meet in heaven.

The judge was not impressed. He ordered jail sentences of sixty days for all the organizers and then said sternly that "Mrs. Jones" would receive a suspended sentence, because she was trying to pose as a martyr. He would not, he said, let her "force her way into jail." However, he warned her that if she were arrested again, she would receive a severe penalty.

Mary had been replaced as strike leader in the northern field when she was arrested. When the trial was over, she returned to the south, to the New River and Kanawha Valley districts. She had no sooner arrived, however, than a judge enjoined her and two other organizers from speaking in public. Injunctions had become the order of the day in the southern field too.

The violence had increased as well. Mary met with the miners only in complete secrecy, under the cover of darkness, in fields, in abandoned mines, in caves. They were all in grave danger. "Men were shot," Mary reported. "They were beaten. Numbers disappeared and no trace of them was found. Storekeepers were ordered not to sell to union men or their families." The organizers often spent their nights hidden in the woods or on the banks of rivers. "We would hear bullets whiz past us," Mary wrote, "as we sat huddled between boulders, our black clothes making us invisible in the blackness of the night."

In Stanaford Mountain, one of the districts Mary visited, the court had issued an injunction forbidding the strikers from going near the mines. When Mary met with the men, they told her that a deputy sheriff had come to arrest them the night before, claiming that someone had seen them "loitering" near the mine entrance. Either he was lying, the men said, or his witness was lying. They hadn't been to the mines at all, and so they had driven the deputy off.

Mary said that the deputy would probably return—with help. She advised the miners to surrender to him when he did, for he would like nothing better than an excuse to use his gun. The miners would be jailed, she knew, but they wouldn't be kept for long. Everyone had to be prepared to spend some time in jail during a strike.

The next morning, Mary was in the village at the foot of the mountain preparing to leave the area when she heard that there had been "trouble on the hill" during the night.

I took the short trail up the hillside. It seemed to me, as I came toward the miners' camp as if those wretched shacks were huddling closer in terror. Everything was deathly still.

As I came near the miners' homes, I could hear sobbing. . . .
I pushed open a door. On a mattress, wet with blood, lay a
miner. . . . In five other shacks men lay dead. In one of them
a baby boy and his mother sobbed over the father's corpse.
The little boy looked up when he saw me. "Mother Jones,"
he cried, "bring back my papa to me!"

The deputy had indeed returned, with a posse of eighty armed
men. They had rushed the camp, some of them shooting as they
went. Eight miners were killed in their beds as they slept and
twenty others were wounded. "The men were buried on the
mountain side," Mary wrote. "And nothing was ever done to
punish the men who had taken their lives."

Although a few of the Stanaford Mountain strikers wished to
hold out, the strike collapsed within a few days of the massacre.
Mary stayed on to console the wives and children of the murdered
men, and to attend the funeral. Then she returned to the Kanawha
Valley.

By the end of the summer, district after district had collapsed
under the weight of company opposition. Some of the strikers had
been blacklisted and could not return to work. But those who
could, did, under the same dangerous conditions, the same long
hours, and the same low wages. By September, the strike was over
in the northern fields. By October, it was over throughout the
state.

In every district except one, the strike had failed completely.
The exception was the Kanawha Valley—to the great credit of
Mary and the other organizers who worked there. An agreement
had been reached guaranteeing the workers a nine-hour work day
and—most important of all—guaranteeing the union the right to
represent them.

Mary left the state soon after the Kanawha Valley agreement was signed. She was not present at the negotiating table where the details were worked out. Important though it was, the conference-table part of union work never appealed to her. She hadn't the patience for it, or the temperament, or the talent.

Although she had worked hard and well in West Virginia, Mary was saddened because so little had been accomplished. Except for the Kanawha Valley, nothing had changed. The miners would suffer and struggle as they had before.

Still, she knew that the defeat of this strike would not be the end of the union in West Virginia. The miners would be ready to try again one day. When they were, she would be there to help them.

"West Virginia," she wrote once in a melancholy mood. "Medieval West Virginia! With its grim men and women. With its tent colonies on the bleak hills. When I get to the other side, I shall tell God Almighty about West Virginia!"

～ NINE ～

THE CHILDREN

Children at work, either beside their parents or at tasks which they could handle alone, was not a new thing in the nineteenth century. Children had always worked on the farm and in the home. But children at work in mines and factories from sunrise to sunset, children who were stoop-shouldered and ill by the time they were ten, and who were commonly crippled on the "job"— that was new, as new as the factory system itself. And in America in the last part of the nineteenth century that was the way over a million children spent their childhood.

These children did not play. They did not go to school. For almost all their waking hours, they worked, shut off from the outside world and cut off from one another. They saw the sky only at dawn as they walked to work, and at dusk as they walked home. These were the children Mary described as "little grey ghosts." If you could see them at work, Mary said, you would see "the most heart-breaking spectacle in all of life."

Mary had seen children at work in the textile factories of the South in the early 1890s. Later, in Pennsylvania, she saw children at work in the coal mines. Some worked as general runners and helpers in the mines. But most were "breaker boys," who had to sift pieces of slate out of the coal as it came pouring down long, steep chutes. Seated on ladders beside the chutes, bent over all day long, their backs were round, their chests narrow. Cut, broken, and crushed fingers were common. If their attention wandered, they were struck across the knuckles by the long stick of the "breaker boss." "The fingers of the little boys bled," Mary said, "onto the coal."

Mary knew how terribly the children of the poor suffered. And the young children who were themselves sent into the mines and mills to work haunted her most of all. In 1903, she thought she saw a chance to do something about it. In that year, in early June, a strike was called by the textile workers in the Kensington mills near Philadelphia. Mary went to help. Sixteen thousand children were counted among the 100,000 strikers. They came into union headquarters in Kensington every day, some with their hands off, some with their thumbs missing, some with their fingers off at the knuckle. Most of them were nine and ten years old.

Mary knew that a law already existed in Pennsylvania prohibiting anyone under the age of thirteen from working in the mills. But no attempt had ever been made to enforce it. Mill owners were happy to hire any child who was big enough to do a job. Children were easy to control, and they were cheap. Parents whose earnings were so low that an extra two or three dollars a

week was a matter of importance sadly sent their children out to work.

The Textile Workers Union had been trying for years to get the Pennsylvania legislature to put some muscle into the law and to get another law passed which would shorten the work day for women and children of the legal age. In the union's formal phrase,

A group of breaker boys.

a shorter day would "prevent their physical and mental deterioration." But the legislature had taken no action.

A few days after Mary arrived at Kensington, she spoke to some newspaper reporters about the children. Why weren't they publicizing the situation, she wanted to know. They couldn't, one reporter responded. The mill owners were partial owners of the newspapers and had "strongly discouraged" them from writing such stories. Besides, he said, everyone knew about child labor. It wasn't really "news."

The following night, at a meeting in union headquarters, Mary announced that she wanted to lead a parade of parents and mill children from Philadelphia's Independence Square to the courthouse lawn, a distance of less than a mile. There they would demonstrate against the mill owners, against child labor, against the do-nothing legislature. They would give the newspapers a story they would have to print.

Early on the morning of June 21, over 300 children and their parents, with Mary in the lead, marched to the courthouse lawn. Mary brought forward those who had been injured or maimed on the job.

"I held up their mutilated hands," she wrote, "some with fingers off, some whose bones had been crushed—and made the statement that Philadelphia's mansions were built on the broken bones, the quivering hearts and drooping heads of these children, that their little lives went out to make wealth for others. I called out to the millionaires to cease their moral murders."

The windows in the huge city hall overlooking the lawn were open. From time to time, Mary could see officials looking out at the crowd. She held the children up for the officials to see. "They were light to lift," she said. But the officials quickly closed their windows, "just as they had closed their hearts." Still, Mary noted with satisfaction the reporters at the fringes of the crowd, hastily counting heads, wandering through the hordes of children, jotting down notes.

She had been right. She had created a newsworthy event. Papers as far away as New York covered the story in the next day's

A young textile worker at the machines.

edition. Some even went beyond describing the demonstration itself to reflect—for a sentence or two—on the problem of child labor. But the day after that, the story was "old news," and so was the issue of child labor.

Mary wanted publicity that would move the government to action. If enough people were concerned, she thought the government would have to do something. The Liberty Bell, usually kept on permanent display in Philadelphia, had just been taken on a tour of the country so that people everywhere could see it. The tour had been a great success, and that gave Mary an idea. She would make a tour of her own: a tour of the mill children. They would march from Kensington to the Long Island summer mansion of the President of the United States, Theodore Roosevelt.

Early in the morning of July 5, at a huge meeting hall in Philadelphia, Mary spoke to the strikers. She told them about the march she wished to conduct, and asked the parents to let their children join it. She would take them to New York in easy stages, she said, averaging ten miles a day and walking only in the cool part of the day. They would bring tents with them, but the children would sleep in farmhouses whenever possible. The marchers would have the use of four wagons, three for provisions and one in which the children could ride if they chose to.

When they came to towns or cities, they would stop and hold demonstrations. Mary would explain who they were, what the strike was about, and where the children were going. Those who could, would play musical instruments. The rest would sing and dance "the usual dances"—the reel, the clog, and the jig. Afterwards, the children would present "little dramas" showing the luxurious and wasteful lives of the rich. Mary planned to take along a sack of fabrics, costume jewelry, and makeup for the children to use in their "theater." And of course, they would "pass the hat" to raise money for the strike fund.

The men and women in the audience voted their approval of Mary's plan by a show of hands. A committee of union men volunteered to help with the preparations and with the march itself.

On the afternoon of July 7, the group set out, about 300 strong, almost 200 of them children between eight and eleven years of age. Most of the people did not plan to make the whole trip, but they wanted to participate in at least the start of the twenty-two-day journey.

The children from the textile mills posing with their signs.

Danny James, eight years old, led the parade out of Kensington. He carried a placard which said, "We Are Textile Workers." Behind him marched one little boy playing a drum, another, a fife, and the rest of the children, who carried flags and posters. "We want more schools and less hospitals," read one sign. "We want time to play," said another. To the tune of "Marching Through Georgia" the group set out for the Bristol Turnpike. Charles Sweeney, a member of the TWU committee, added a touch of style as he marched alongside the children twirling his red, white, and blue baton.

The hot July sun baked the marchers as they walked along. The older people held up umbrellas to shield themselves from it, and the children took off their coats and hats and loosened their collars. By the time they reached the turnpike, the heat was blistering. Mary sent most of the girls ahead by trolley, and she rode on the wagon with some of the younger boys.

At six o'clock that night they all met, as planned, at Torresdale Park, on the outskirts of Philadelphia, about halfway between Kensington and Bristol. The grounds looked like the site of a "gigantic picnic," as everyone rested, looking forward to the evening meal. The committee gave each marcher a tin cup, a dinner plate, and a spoon. The adults set out huge platters of bread and cheese which they had brought with them; bowls of fruit and vegetables were donated by local farmers.

One thousand people came to the park grounds later that night to meet the marchers and to hear Mary speak. A total of $76.40 was collected for the strike fund. Everything went well, and spirits were high—though there were a few unscheduled happenings. A man and a boy were expelled from the group for jumping a fence and chasing some chickens. Three eleven-year-old boys confessed that they had not actually received permission to join the march and were sent home.

The next morning, after a breakfast of sandwiches, coffee, and ice cream, the group assembled. Sweeney and Mary thought that the heat was more than some of the children could stand. Those children, along with other children and adults who had planned to come only this far, returned to Philadelphia. At eleven o'clock, the remaining marchers, now numbering fewer than 100, set off down the road. The farmers who had contributed food the day before saw them off.

By the middle of the afternoon they had arrived in Bristol. But the police kept them from entering the city until Mary persuaded them that the group was orderly and did not intend to cause a disturbance. After resting near a brook that ran outside the west end of town, the group entered the city proper. Band playing and banners waving, they marched through the streets giving out flyers which announced "A Speech to Be Given by Mother Jones, Entitled: The Abolition of Child Labor and the Causes of the Textile Workers Strike in Philadelphia."

Two thousand people gathered that night to hear Mary speak. They cheered her warmly, and when a collection was taken up, they contributed generously. Mrs. Jennie Silbert of the Silbert Hotel invited Mary and the women and children to spend the night with her.

The next morning, some more adult members of the group departed for Kensington—one complaining about Mary's leadership and the others having lost interest in the march altogether. But the rest, refreshed and in good spirits, set out for Morrisville on the banks of the Delaware River. Just outside of town, a few of the boys "broke ranks" to bathe and swim in the fresh blue water.

Soon dusty clothing and dust-covered banners hung from the branches of trees up and down the riverbank as the march came to an unscheduled but delightful stop. "I think," Mary reported to union headquarters, "that never again will the children have a holiday to equal this. . . . They are very happy."

The next day, the group pushed on for Trenton. But when they got to the Delaware River Bridge that led into the city, they were told that they would have to pay a toll of two cents per person. Mary lined the marchers up by twos, so they would be easier to count. They numbered fifty-two now, and Mary carefully paid out $1.04. Then she told the astonished bridge-keeper that she thought it was outrageous to charge people for crossing a bridge! (She also told him that she didn't blame him personally. She understood that he had his job to do, just like everyone else. But it was a shame that he had to be "an instrument of injustice.")

From Trenton, where they were forbidden to play instruments as they marched along, the group moved on to Princeton. They were still on the road when a fierce rainstorm began. Chilled and miserable, they huddled in and under the wagons and among the trees. Fortunately, the storm passed as quickly as it had come, and in the high hot sun of the afternoon, the group's spirits revived.

Princeton University was nearby, and early the next morning, Mary received an invitation to speak to an economics class. She accepted the invitation and took with her James Ashworth, a ten-year-old boy.

"Here's a textbook in economics," she said, pointing to the child. "He is stooped over because his spine is curved from carrying, day after day, bundles of yarn that weigh seventy-five pounds. He gets three dollars a week and his sister, who is

fourteen, gets six dollars. They work in a carpet factory ten hours
a day while the children of the rich"—she paused to look at the
audience—"while the children of the rich are getting their higher
education."

By this time a number of children looked run-down and exhausted. She sent them home, accompanied by two of the women.
The rest moved on to the Raritan River, across from New Brunswick, and set up camp on a hillside. On the second night, there
was another heavy rainstorm—and some complaints from the
adults. A *New York Times* reporter found them there. "They
looked tired and disgusted with the whole thing," he wrote. A half
dozen men left the group, one of them complaining to the re-

Mary and the children march through a town in New Jersey.

porter, "It's all right for Mother Jones. She sleeps in a hotel. I would rather work sixty hours a day than endure this torture."

Mary did not comment on the man's complaint. They all slept indoors when they could. It was true that shelter was offered Mary and the children more often than it was offered the men. But given her age and the rigors of the march, the complaint was petty and she could not take it seriously.

In Rahway the next evening, the group received permission to hold a meeting. A member of the TWU committee stood on a chair in the middle of the street which had been roped off for them and introduced Mary to a crowd of over 1,000 people.

She climbed onto the chair ("without any help," a local newspaper thought it worth mentioning). "Friends and enemies," she began, "for it is clear that the children have both." To warm applause and cries of "Hear! Hear!" Mary accused the nation's industrialists of "crucifying little children," employing them because they were cheap labor, and growing rich at their expense. She ended her speech by pledging to continue the march until the group reached the President's door. If something could be done for the children, she said, "it would be a blessing not only for them but for the whole nation."

The next day, in Elizabeth, a friendly press welcomed the marchers and described Mary as "the greatest female agitator in the country . . . an intelligent woman, a great thinker and a forceful speaker." That night a cheerful crowd greeted the children warmly and applauded Mary for several minutes when she got up to speak. (Midway through the speech, the "forceful speaker" interrupted herself to snap at a man in the front row who was puffing away on a cigar, sending clouds of smoke into her face.

"Take that scab cigar out of your mug!" Mary demanded. He did.)

The next morning, two businessmen welcomed Mary and invited her to take an automobile ride. It was her first. She was delighted with the "contraption," and the three toured the city in friendly high spirits. That afternoon, Mary wrote a letter to President Roosevelt, urging him to make a personal commitment to America's children. "We ask you, Mr. President," she wrote, "if our commercial greatness has not cost us too much by being built on the quivering hearts of helpless children. . . . We . . . are now marching toward you in the hope that your tender heart will counsel with us to abolish this crime."

Soon reports appeared in the newspapers describing the President's response to Mary's letter. According to his private secretary, William Barnes, the President "would probably be willing to meet Mother Jones if she made a request in the usual formal way," but he objected to "having his castle stormed." Barnes added that the President had ordered extra police to the mansion to prevent that from happening.

Mary was skeptical. She doubted whether Barnes's comments really reflected the President's thoughts. When reporters asked her if the group would continue to Oyster Bay, she replied that they would. What was more, she thought the President would see them—"if he is the President of all the people and not just of the industrialists."

Meanwhile the group pushed on to Hoboken and then Passaic, just across the river from New York. There Mary received some news that deeply upset her. The President's Secret Service had been keeping the march under surveillance. Union officials as well as reporters confirmed the story, and Mary had to accept its truth. Nevertheless, she excused the President for any part he might have played. She told reporters that she believed he had not been shown her letter at all, but had just been told that "an old agitator named Mother Jones wanted to come and make a scene and plague him." She wished the President to see the children, she said, because if he met them, and compared them with his own children who were spending the summer at play on the seashore, perhaps he would be moved to help them.

On July 22, the group held its last campfire on the Jersey City Heights. Mary had gone into New York early in the morning to apply for a parade permit. Turned away by the New York City police commissioner, she went over his head to the mayor, Seth Low. After much wrangling, during which Mary pointed out in heated tones that New York had given an honored welcome to Prince Henry of Germany, "a piece of rotten royalty," the mayor granted the permit. The next morning, July 23, the marchers crossed the Hudson River into Manhattan on the Christopher Street Ferry. From there they walked to the headquarters of the Social Democratic party, at 64 East 4th Street, a six-story building in the heart of the tenement district. The Social Democratic party had given the marchers the use of their rooms for as long as they would be in the city.

In the evening, the group began its march to East 27th Street, one block from Madison Square, where they would hold a meeting.

Playing drums and fifes and carrying torches, the group, now about sixty strong, proceeded up Fourth Avenue. Hundreds of policemen lined the route, and thousands of New Yorkers cheered as the youngsters passed by. Mary walked at the head of the group, smiling and waving at the people, while the other adults brought up the rear. Almost 30,000 people had gathered at the intersection of Madison and 27th Street, where the group stopped. Mary and three of the children climbed aboard a wagon draped in red. The leader of the Social Democratic party addressed the people first. Then he introduced Mary, who came forward with the children. She introduced the audience to Gussie Rangnew and Joseph Ashford, children "from whom all the childhood has gone." She introduced Eddie Dunphy, "a little fellow of twelve whose job is to sit all day on a high stool handing in the right thread to other workers, eleven hours a day, all day long, winter and summer, spring and fall, for three dollars a week." The children sat down and Mary spoke softly to the huge crowd. "We are marching quietly to the President's home," she said. "I believe he can do something for these children, though the press declares he cannot."

The marchers' headquarters on East 4th Street attracted curious onlookers from all over the city. "East Side girls" came, Mary said, "with their short skirts, tilted hats and iron-clad assurance." Youngsters came, too, eager to see the children who were "being tooken to see Ruzevelt." Mary herself was visited by some men who claimed to belong to the President's Secret Service. They told her not to go to Oyster Bay. She was skeptical of their credentials and told them so. In any case, she said, even if they did represent the U.S. government, she represented the Philadelphia textile workers. They had every right to see the President and she intended for them to do so.

That evening the group marched again to their meeting place on 27th Street and Madison Avenue. But this time the site was blocked by twelve police officers, headed by Inspector J. Walsh.

As the group approached, Inspector Walsh stepped forward. He explained to Mary in friendly tones that he had been ordered to move the group to a site a few blocks farther east. Then he and a sergeant offered to walk arm in arm with Mary, as an escort of honor.

In her speech, Mary ad-libbed a bit more than usual to include a word about the New York police. She said that if things went well, and she got to see the President, she would tell him how hard the police had to work "to prevent the cries of a demoralized country." And she would ask him to shorten their work day to eight hours. Then, returning to the main topic, she made two points at the same time. "If children weren't stultified by slavery and were sent to school instead," she said, "you police officers wouldn't have so much work to do."

The next day the group went to Coney Island as the guests of Mr. Frank Bostock, the owner of a wild animal show. The children swam in the ocean, played on the beach, and helped the animal keepers tend and feed the animals. One child told a reporter from *The New York Times* that he never wanted to go back to the mill. He wanted to stay and "live with the circus."

That evening, a crowd gathered to hear Mary speak. "We want the President to hear the wail of the children who never have a chance to go to school but work from ten to twelve hours a day in the textile mills of Philadelphia, weaving the carpets you and he walk on. Fifty years ago," she continued, "there was a cry against slavery and men gave up their lives to stop the selling of black children on the block. Today the white child is sold for two dollars a week to the manufacturers."

When Mary finished speaking, she stepped back and took a seat beside the children while the hat was passed around. She was tired, and she knew the others were tired too. They had been on the road for almost four weeks, and though people everywhere had been kind and generous, the trip had taken its toll. Mary wanted them all to get a good night's rest, especially since the next day might find them at Oyster Bay. First, she said, they would stop at the Oriental Hotel in exclusive Manhattan Beach, a few miles away. New York's Senator Platt was staying there and had agreed to see them if they could come first thing in the morning. He might be persuaded to put in a good word about them to the President.

The group rose early and the children went swimming before starting out. It was a gay and noisy procession. Mary and the other men and women walked quietly enough, but the children crowded around an elephant which Bostock had given them for the trip. He had fitted the animal with a howdah and some of the children rode in it.

Perhaps the circus atmosphere frightened Senator Platt. Or perhaps he had already changed his mind and decided not to meet with the marchers. In any event, when the group arrived, Mary was told that the Senator had slipped out the back door "in a big rush."

Though she was a bit amused at the thought of the dignified Senator fleeing, she was also very angry. She told the marchers and the reporters who had accompanied them from Coney Island to come inside. They all had breakfast, and on Mary's instructions, the waiters put the tab on the Senator's bill.

Afterwards, somewhat stymied, Mary led the group back to the beach where the children could play while she and the union committee decided what to do next. For the last leg of the journey, the trip to Oyster Bay itself, Mary said she wanted only three children to accompany her, and two union men and their wives. The President might refuse to see even so modest a delegation, but at least they would try. Those who would not be coming returned to Manhattan to wait while the others prepared to go to Oyster Bay.

The next day, the little group arrived at the President's mansion. They were stopped at the gate, where Secretary Barnes came out to speak to them.

The President would not see them. "He has nothing to do with child labor," Barnes explained, and could not help them "in their struggle for better conditions." He advised Mary to submit what she had to say "in writing." With that he turned and walked away.

The group returned quietly to Manhattan.

By the end of the week, the others had made arrangements for the return trip to Philadelphia. Mary had decided to remain in New York for a while longer with the three children who had gone with her to Oyster Bay. She wrote to the President and did not want to leave until she received an answer. Perhaps the President would agree to see them after all.

In a few days, Mary got her answer. It was from Secretary Barnes. He said that the children had the President's sympathy, but that he had no power to do anything for them. The matter was in the hands of the individual states and of the Congress.

Mary was not surprised at the President's response, but she was deeply disappointed. His presence alone, the respect he commanded, could persuade people—citizens and lawmakers alike—to look more closely at the problem. Legislation would surely follow. But he had refused to consider the issue. He would not become involved. In that regard, the march had failed to accomplish what Mary had hoped it would.

In other ways, however, Mary knew that the march had done a great deal of good. No one who had seen the children would ever forget them. And the children themselves were aware, as they had not been before, that what was happening to them was not fair, not natural. It did not happen to all children. The seeds of reform had been planted. Someday soon they would surely begin to grow.

♘ TEN ♘

COLORADO:
THE FIRST TIME

In the fall of 1903, the last of the children returned to Kensington, and Mary left Pennsylvania for a visit with Eugene Debs in Indiana. Mary knew that Debs was deeply involved in politics now. He had formed his own political party after the defeat of his American Railway Union almost ten years before.

The union had been crushed by the federal government, which had issued an injunction forbidding all strike activities, and backed up the injunction with 50,000 federal soldiers. The special federal attorney who ordered the injunction, Edwin Walker, claimed it was necessary because the railroads were a "public highway," and that if workers quit as a group, they were "conspiring to interfere with commerce." But Debs and the workers knew that Walker had been a lawyer for the railroad before he was appointed to his federal position. And they knew that the man who appointed him, Attorney General Richard Olney, had also been a railroad lawyer before becoming Attorney General. Olney was still a member of the board of several railroad lines. It was clear that he and Walker had used their positions and the law to help the railroad corporations crush the strike. The whole affair had convinced Debs that the government represented the "capitalists," the owners and employers, not the workers. In any conflict, he felt, the government would always take the capitalists' side. If the working people were ever to gain their rights, the government itself would have to change. So Debs had gone into politics.

Debs wanted America to become a "socialist" country. He wanted the state itself, not individual citizens, to own the basic industries—the railroads, communications, and the mines. He thought private owners ran industries for their own benefit. But the state would run the industries for the benefit of all the people.

Mary believed in socialism in theory, because it promised a future in which there would be justice for the working class. But she could not focus on the future—while people faced terrible problems in the present. Although over the years she often supported Debs and the Socialist party he formed, the only organizations she ever worked closely with were the ones which aimed to help the workers in the present: the unions. "Socialism is a long way off," she said once. "I want something now." And at times she was sharply critical of the socialists, accusing them of being "too sentimental" and of dreaming dreams so lofty and fine that they did not hear "the groans and heartaches of the people."

But now, in the rambling old house in Terre Haute, there were only good feelings as Debs congratulated Mary on the children's march and told her about his own plans for the upcoming 1904 presidential election. He was going to run for President on the Socialist party ticket, as he had in 1900. He did not expect to win the election, but he knew that a national campaign was an opportunity to bring the ideas of socialism to a great many people.

The days passed peacefully, and it was with reluctance that Mary prepared to leave. But she was anxious to get to UMW headquarters in Indianapolis and find out the latest news from President John Mitchell. She had been out of touch for quite a while and was eager to be brought up to date.

The news Mitchell had for Mary was about Colorado. The UMW had been working there, off and on, since the 1890s. So had another union, the Western Federation of Miners, whose members were metal miners. Both had conducted major drives in the winter and spring of 1902–1903, and had managed to establish a number of strong local branches. Their main concern was to shorten the work day, which was as long as twelve hours for most miners. An eight-hour law had been passed by the Colorado legislature, but the state supreme court, under pressure from the mine owners, had declared it unconstitutional. At that, the WFM had called a strike, and now was urging the UMW to join it in a united, statewide walkout of all miners.

Mitchell was worried. He needed more information about the entire area before he could decide whether or not the UMW should join the strike. He asked Mary to go to Colorado to find out exactly what the situation was. How many workers would support a strike? How bad were conditions? What would the opposition be like?

Mary arrived in Trinidad, in southern Colorado, on October 26, 1903. Checking into a small hotel, she registered simply as "M. Jones, Chicago." She had told no one of her arrival and did not want any publicity. Still, the news got out. She was a well-known woman now, and many people were curious about her.

Mary in a formal photograph, c. 1904.

Within a few hours the lobby was crowded with men and women—police deputies and mine company officials as well as workers—who wanted to get a glimpse of her. But they had to settle for a look at her signature in the hotel register, for Mary had already been in and out.

She had no sooner closed the door to her room than she changed from her usual black dress and conservative bonnet into an old calico dress and a broad sunbonnet. Then, swinging a case full of pins and needles, swatches of fabric, knives, and forks, she went out. Anyone who saw her would think she was an old peddler. Disguised this way, she could go where she pleased.

Over the next few weeks, Mary traveled throughout the area surrounding Trinidad. All the coal fields in southern Colorado— almost a half-million acres of land—were owned by two companies: the Colorado Fuel and Iron Company under John D. Rockefeller, and the Victor-America Company under Jay Gould. Mary made her way through the district, knocking on doors, staying for a cup of tea, seeing how the people who worked for the giant coal companies lived. She did not have to be told about their poverty. She saw the company-owned houses, crumbling one-room shacks with bare dirt floors and broken windows. She saw the children who did not have enough to eat, who suffered from every kind of illness. Several families told her that company officials entered and searched their homes anytime they wanted to. They told her about armed guards who threatened and beat anyone who objected to company policies. She learned of dozens of men who had been fired because they would not buy at the company store, and others who were driven from the area because they were thought to have joined the union.

One of the bitterest complaints was about the way the miners were paid. Their wages depended on the amount of coal they dug. It was weighed at the end of each day—by company weighmen, and the miners were not allowed to check the measurement. Often they were cheated, and they knew it. In addition, they were paid in scrip, not cash, so they had no choice but to buy everything they needed from the company stores. Here, as in West Virginia, the company stores charged the highest prices of any stores in the district. The miners of Colorado, Mary concluded, lived in "practical" if not legal slavery. She sent word to Mitchell that a strike was not only in order, it was long past due.

Mitchell was reluctant. The Western Federation of Miners had begun to recruit coal miners as well as metal miners, and in some ways was more a rival than a friend of his union, the United Mine Workers. It was a far more militant organization, and he did not get along with its leaders. In addition, the miners in the southern part of the state were almost all recent immigrants—Italian, Polish, and Greek. They spoke very little English and would be difficult to work with.

In the end, though, Mitchell found the reports from Mary and other investigators overwhelming. On November 9, the strike began. Coal miners and their families, carrying all that they owned—dishes, blankets, clothing—moved out of their cabins and into the hills, into tents which the union had provided. Though the strike was statewide, Mary chose to remain in the south, where the workers were poorest, and where the opposition from the Rockefeller and Gould companies could be expected to be strong. She had made solid connections with WFM organizers

Company houses in Colorado. Train tracks for the coal cars run right beside them.

who had established a stronghold in the Cripple Creek area, and she was prepared to work with them as well as with the other UMW organizers.

As the strike began, the cold mountain winter began too. The families in their tents on the hillsides shivered and huddled together. Mary traveled from camp to camp, bringing news and encouragement, food and medical supplies. She set up a distribution center in Trinidad stocked with medicines, clothing, and food purchased by the union. When she had the use of a wagon, she loaded it herself and traveled to the isolated tent colonies, often staying overnight with one of the families. Just her presence was a comfort.

The strike was only a few weeks old when Mary heard that the coal companies in the north had offered to settle with their employees. The mining companies were unwilling to accept the union as the miners' official representative, but they did agree to a wage increase and to an eight-hour day. It wasn't the best offer, but it was a good one, and under other circumstances, Mary might have been pleased. But not now. If the northern miners settled, and the southern miners were left to carry on the strike alone, they would surely be defeated. They had begun the strike together, and, Mary thought, when the time came, they should settle together.

John Mitchell did not agree. Rumor had it that he was urging the northern workers to accept the offer. A meeting had been called for the twenty-first of November in the northern town of Louisville. There the miners would vote on the companies' offer.

Mary left for Louisville as soon as she heard about the meeting, traveling with William Howells, president of the UMW's Trinidad local. They arrived just in time for the meeting, and learned that a telegram from Mitchell had come that afternoon. In it he urged the northern miners to accept the settlement and end their strike, and he asked all UMW organizers to help persuade them to do so.

At the meeting, Howells spoke first. He asked the miners to offer the companies a "conditional agreement": they would accept the offer and return to work if and when the southern companies offered a similar settlement to their workers. According to a reporter from the Denver *Post*, Howells was courteously received. But when he was finished, there were loud calls for Mother Jones.

Mary addressed herself straightforwardly to Mitchell's telegram. In comments which shocked "good members" of the union, she dismissed the president's recommendation as worthless. "A general," she said, "cannot give orders unless he is in the field, unless he is at the battleground." Then, looking intently at the miners in the audience, she paused.

"Are you brave men?" she asked in her low, strong voice. "Can you fight as well as you can work? If you go back to work here and your brothers fall in the south, you will be responsible for their defeat. . . ."

Some angry voices were heard from the back of the room, but they were soon drowned out by earnest cries of "Tell us, Mother!"

"I don't know what you will do," Mary continued, "but I know very well what I would do if I were in one of your places. . . . I would say we will all go to Glory together or we will die and go down together. We must stand together; if we don't, there will be no victory for any one of us."

The effect, the reporter said, was "electrical." There was prolonged applause and cheering, and many miners stood up to honor

Mary. Then the vote was taken: the northern miners turned down the settlement, defying Mitchell's urgings.

Mary went back to the south, pleased with the vote. Though she was still an official representative of the UMW, she let it be known that she would work with anyone who was committed to helping the strikers—meaning, of course, that she would work with the WFM if the UMW began to back away.

Mitchell was very disturbed. He was convinced that the northerners must settle. Their gesture of unity with the southerners—at Mary's instigation—was both foolish and futile. Under his instructions, organizers asked the miners in the north to reconsider. There was no point in holding out for the southerners. Rockefeller and Gould might never be persuaded to settle. The northern companies had made a good offer, and the miners should accept it and return to work.

A week after the original meeting, another vote was taken. This time, the settlement was accepted. The date was November 30.

Almost immediately, Mary's fears were confirmed, as the southern companies stepped up their efforts to squelch the strike in the south. Additional armed guards were hired, and under their protection, strikebreakers from out of the state were brought in. Strikers were kept away at gunpoint.

But the guards did not restrict themselves to "strikebreaker duty." They were encouraged by the companies to "let the strikers know who was boss," and they did, with a brutal show of force. Strikers were ambushed if they walked alone. Families were terrorized by guards who pretended to be looking for stolen supplies and in the process ransacked their shelters and destroyed their possessions. Children were threatened and chased when they went out to play. The strikers began to arm themselves and to fight back. Mitchell, at UMW headquarters in Indianapolis, began to wonder whether the southern strikers shouldn't surrender.

By the end of December, a month after the northern agreement, southern Colorado was said to be in a "state of revolt." Governor James J. Peabody declared martial law. The militiamen and their commanders did not even try to disguise the fact that, in their eyes, strikers were criminals, or that they considered the very presence of union organizers a menace to the peace. They arrested people at will and detained them for as long as they liked without trial or hearing.

Strikers were picked up for "loitering" and forced to work on chain gangs in freezing temperatures. So many people were arrested that special "bullpens" were built, open stockades into which prisoners were herded like so many cattle.

Many people who were not involved in the strike themselves were shocked at the troops' actions. A group of businessmen and other citizens sent a letter of protest to the governor. In a dramatic bid to publicize the terrors of the military rule under which they were living, the WFM designed a poster showing an American flag above the caption: "Is Colorado in America?" Their organizers were arrested for "defiling the flag of the United States." When one reporter suggested to J. P. McClelland, the commander of the state militia, that his orders were unconstitutional, he answered: "To hell with the Constitution. We are not going by the Constitution. We are following the orders of Governor Peabody."

Under military law, public meetings could be held and speeches given only with the express consent of the military authorities. Mary personally was warned that if her speeches "inspired rebel-

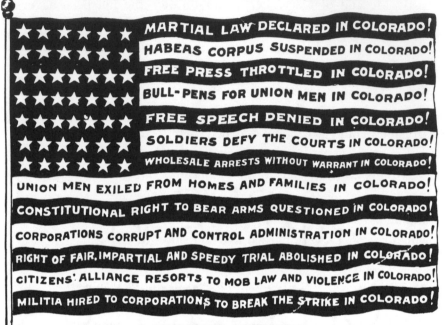

IS COLORADO IN AMERICA ?

MARTIAL LAW DECLARED IN COLORADO!
HABEAS CORPUS SUSPENDED IN COLORADO!
FREE PRESS THROTTLED IN COLORADO!
BULL-PENS FOR UNION MEN IN COLORADO!
FREE SPEECH DENIED IN COLORADO!
SOLDIERS DEFY THE COURTS IN COLORADO!
WHOLESALE ARRESTS WITHOUT WARRANT IN COLORADO!
UNION MEN EXILED FROM HOMES AND FAMILIES IN COLORADO!
CONSTITUTIONAL RIGHT TO BEAR ARMS QUESTIONED IN COLORADO!
CORPORATIONS CORRUPT AND CONTROL ADMINISTRATION IN COLORADO!
RIGHT OF FAIR, IMPARTIAL AND SPEEDY TRIAL ABOLISHED IN COLORADO!
CITIZENS' ALLIANCE RESORTS TO MOB LAW AND VIOLENCE IN COLORADO!
MILITIA HIRED TO CORPORATIONS TO BREAK THE STRIKE IN COLORADO!

THESE are absolute facts and are not the only outrages that have been perpetrated in Colorado in the name of law and order. It has been charged and never successfully denied that the corporations contributed $15,000.00 towards the election of the present Republican administration, but Governor Peabody has been unable to "DELIVER THE GOODS."

THE unions have not been nor can they be abolished, and before the strikes in Colorado are settled, we will have demonstrated the right to organize for mutual benefit. The eight-hour day as decreed by over forty thousand majority of the voters will be established.

IF you desire to assist the striking Miners, Mill and Smeltermen of the Western Federation of Miners of Colorado in this battle for industrial and political freedom, send donations to Wm. D Haywood, Sec'y-Treas. 625 Mining Exchange Denver, Colorado.

Charles Moyer
PRESIDENT

Wm D Haywood
SEC Y-TREAS

Western Federation of Miners' poster protesting conditions in Colorado.

lion," she would be arrested. But in the month of January she did not give any speeches. She was hospitalized in Trinidad with pneumonia.

Her illness should not have been surprising. She was, after all, seventy-three years old, traveling the snow-covered roads, sleeping in tents, subject to wind, rain, and freezing temperatures. She worked in ways and places that would have drained the strength of healthy people half her age. Still, her illness was a shock, for she had an aura of strength around her which was legendary.

Reporters noted the strikers' grave concern for a woman they had come to love. "Everywhere one goes in Trinidad," one correspondent wrote, "groups of miners can be seen, waiting for the latest news about Mother Jones. I myself could not walk far without someone stopping me to ask, in trembling tones and broken English, 'Mudder Jones . . . she is well yet?' "

Mary's enemies made themselves heard at this time too. Late in January, an article about her appeared in a Denver weekly newspaper called *Polly Pry*. The article claimed that the woman "whom the wives and children of the deluded miners called 'Mother' was in fact a vulgar, heartless creature with a fiery temper and a cold-blooded brutality." Mrs. George Anthony, the writer and also the founder of the paper, claimed that Mary's battle cry was: "We'd rather fight than work!"—a malicious twist of what Mary had said to the northern miners in Louisville when she urged them not to agree to a separate settlement. "Are you brave men?" she had asked. "Can you fight as well as you can work?"

The article went on to claim that Mary was anything but the "people's champion" she was often thought to be. She had, according to Mrs. Anthony, lived a low and sordid life as a prostitute in and around Colorado before going to work for the miners' union. What motivated Mary to become an organizer? Mrs. Anthony thought the answer was simple: Mary wanted power. She already "owned and controlled the United Mine Workers of America and that sister organization, the Western Federation of Miners," the article stated, and now "Mother Jones sighs for new worlds to conquer." Specifically, Mary was said to be after "political ownership of the state of Colorado."

Many newspapers picked up the story the next day, and the next week *Polly Pry* ran another article about Mary. Added to the list of charges was Mary's "habitual drunkenness," several "arrests for disorderly conduct," and an underworld boyfriend named "Black Leg."

Mary did not try to defend herself. Though the stories became well known, they were not widely believed, and they did not hurt her relationship with the miners or with any of the people she tried to help. Perhaps she felt that if she became involved in a quarrel with Mrs. Anthony, the publicity would focus even more attention on the charges. Many years later, she explained to the journalist Upton Sinclair that the prostitute charge had not come entirely as a surprise to her. It dated back to the 1880s, when Mary had befriended a prostitute in Chicago. The woman had died and been refused burial in a Catholic cemetery. Mary had written to a local newspaper condemning the Church for its action. In return, she herself had been accused of being a prostitute.

In any case, when Mrs. Anthony made the charges, Mary did not answer them at all. John Mitchell wanted her to sue the newspaper, and an attorney for the UMW began to study the

Colorado laws regarding slander. But he concluded that they were very weak and that it was unlikely that Mary would win her case. The matter was dropped.

Mary left the hospital in February. Soon her small, familiar figure was once again on the streets of Trinidad and the roads of Cripple Creek, as often as not with a group of children at her heels. In March, she spoke at a mass meeting of miners on the western outskirts of Trinidad. The meeting went smoothly, and there were no disruptions. But the next night, a few minutes after midnight, soldiers burst into Mary's room and ordered her to come with them.

"I always slept in my clothes," she remarked calmly, "for I never knew what might happen."

She was held in military headquarters until dawn, when she and three other organizers were placed on a train heading for La Junta, Colorado, sixty-five miles northeast of Trinidad. There they were put off and told never to return to Colorado.

Mary spent the night in La Junta, but the next morning she returned to the train yard. She chatted with several workers until she found a conductor who expressed strong sympathy with the Colorado miners. Impressed at learning that the old woman with whom he was speaking was *the* Mother Jones, he quickly agreed to put her on a train for Denver. So, back she went.

Arriving in the capital, she checked into a hotel and wrote a message to Governor Peabody. She had no intention of obeying a nameless, formless military order. "I wish to notify you, Governor," she went on, "that you don't own the state of Colorado. When it was admitted to the sisterhood of states, my fathers gave me a share of stock in it, and that is all they gave to you. . . . I am right here in the capital. . . . 4 or 5 blocks from your office. And I want to ask you, Governor, what in Hell are you going to do about it?"

The governor did nothing about it, and the next day Mary left Denver to travel through the southern district, holding meetings and rallies. But no sooner did she return to Trinidad than she got the governor's answer. She was immediately arrested and placed on a train bound for Utah.

It was April now. Mary knew the authorities were watching her, and, rather than return to Trinidad only to be deported again, she decided to remain in the town of Helper for a while, a little town on the Colorado-Utah border. She would help the metal miners there, members of the WFM who had joined the strike.

Mary was invited to live with an Italian family in the strikers' tent colony. When the sheriff told her that she would not be allowed to speak in the town itself, she held a meeting in a flat dry "no-man's land" just beyond the town limits. It was a bleak setting, but Mary rallied and encouraged the miners, reminding them that they had a right to strike—that justice was on their side, and that they must hold out. "This nation," she said under a brooding Utah sky, "was founded on a strike. . . . Washington struck against King George and we will strike against King Gould."

The next day, "King Gould" answered—in the person of the Utah health authorities. Suddenly, it seemed, the board of health discovered that Mary had been exposed to smallpox. She was hustled away and placed in a small shack on the outskirts of town. The door was locked from the outside, a "quarantine" sign was hung, and Mary was left alone.

Her friends among the miners did not leave her there for long.

Under "mysterious" circumstances, the shack caught fire during the night. Mary was "rescued" and taken back to the tent colony.

The next day passed quietly enough. Then at midnight, a squad of mine guards entered the camp, headed by the sheriff. With torches blazing and guns drawn, they went from tent to tent, pulling people out of bed, herding them into the center of the colony. There they read a list of 120 names, people who were under arrest for having broken "quarantine rules."

As their names were called out, some of the miners ran to hide in the hills. But most submitted to arrest and were taken away to the county jail. "Not one law had these miners broken," Mary recalled. "The pitiful screams of the women and children would have penetrated heaven."

Mary herself was placed under arrest and kept in confinement for almost two weeks.

Throughout this time, John Mitchell had done what he thought was reasonable to help the southern strikers. He had urged President Roosevelt to intervene. He had seen to it that some money was sent to the strikers. But by May, he was persuaded that the effort in southern Colorado was entirely useless. He notified the strikers that they ought to surrender. In any case, he announced, as of July 1, they would receive no more funds from the union.

Mary returned to Colorado from Utah in early June. She found the UMW organizers demoralized. They complained bitterly about Mitchell's conduct throughout the strike. Now he was about to abandon them altogether. The WFM remained committed. Its leaders would stay for as long as the strike lasted. But as the summer wore on, and the violence continued, defeat was in the air. In one final act of malice, mine guards destroyed the strikers' food center. They broke in, "looted . . . and ripped open sacks of flour and sugar . . . and poured kerosene over everything," Mary reported.

In mid-July Mary was once again arrested and forced out of the area. An eyewitness who saw her being led from her hotel by rifle-bearing soldiers was outraged that they would march "a white-haired old woman like Mother Jones" at gunpoint. But the "white-haired old woman" had been the moving force in the southern Colorado strike. If the intention of the authorities was to further weaken the spirit of the miners, to show them that they were beaten, marching Mother Jones along the street at gunpoint was a well-chosen tactic.

By October, with the promise of another cold winter coming, it was all over. The miners returned to the Rockefeller and Gould mines, to the company houses, the company stores, and a work day still twelve—and in some cases fourteen—hours long. Mary, back in the southern Colorado coal fields, stayed with the miners until the end. She praised them for their courage, and she tried to comfort them in their defeat.

Mary didn't speak to the miners about her anger toward John Mitchell, but she blamed him for what had happened. In a speech she gave in New York a few months later, Mary said the union's leaders had "remained in their rooms" when they should have been "out in the field watching the pirates." Mitchell himself, Mary noted bitterly, had gone on a trip to Europe during the strike. The fact that he had gone to meet with European unionists and attend a series of conferences did not impress her. "The southern miners," she wrote later, "went out on the bleak mountainsides, lived in tents through a horrible winter with 18 inches of snow on the ground. They tied their feet in gunny sacks and lived lean and lank and hungry as timber wolves. They received 63¢ a week in strike benefits while John Mitchell went traveling through Europe, staying at fashionable hotels, studying the labor movement."

John Mitchell, in his turn, blamed Mary and the other southern organizers for not realizing much earlier that the strike could not be won. He noted that when Mary went to urge the northern miners not to settle, "she disregarded the advice given her." He was displeased enough to add that if Mary "expected to be employed by us she must carry out the orders of the National Board."

Mitchell insisted that in spite of Mary's "insubordination," she would always have a place in the UMW. Shortly after the Colorado strike, however, Mary resigned from the union. For a time she worked with Eugene Debs and the Socialist party. Although later she would work for the UMW again, she never fully regained her respect for its president. "I know whatever mistakes he has made," she said, "he is right at heart." But she never forgave his "mistakes," and at the end of her life she accused him of having "made a profession out of labor" and of having forgotten the workers in his desire to advance himself.

Mary was not alone in her criticism of Mitchell. He was forced to resign the presidency of the UMW in 1908, under heavy criticism for not being "militant" enough in his dealings with the corporations. Still, there is no doubt that Mary and Mitchell were both devoted people. The conflicts between them were, as Clarence Darrow noted, the age-old conflicts between people of thought and people of action. Mitchell was a negotiator. He could spend days, weeks, at the planning board and the conference table. He could calculate and balance one group against another, future gains against present losses. He could haggle and he could compromise.

To Mary, the issue was always justice, an issue on which she would not compromise. The workers were not asking for kindness or mercy. They were asking for things they were entitled to have, things which were due them. In the conflict between owners and workers, she saw a single simple theme: some people were denying the human rights of others. Settlements which contained concessions were not acceptable to her. To compromise with injustice, she felt, was to allow it to continue.

✦ ELEVEN ✦

DEFENDING "MURDERERS" AND "ALIENS"

On a windy day in December, 1905, Frank Steunenberg, governor of Idaho, opened his front gate and was killed by a bomb which had been planted there.

Four weeks later in Colorado, three men were seized, secretly placed aboard a special train, and taken under armed guard to Idaho. There they were arrested and charged with Governor Steunenberg's murder. Almost as soon as newspapers printed the story, Mary was on her way to the Idaho State Penitentiary to see them. She was convinced that they had been "set up," and she was determined to help them.

Mary was sure the men were not guilty because she knew them. They were labor leaders, associated with the WFM, and Mary had met them during the Colorado strike. The governor's actions during a brutal strike in Idaho had earned him the hatred

155

of unionists, particularly WFM members; but Mary felt that these men would not use murder as a tactic.

William, "Big Bill," Haywood was the most famous of the defendants. He was also the one Mary knew best. He was a giant of a man, born and raised in the rough-and-tumble mining towns of the West. He had been a cowboy, he had homesteaded his own land, he had worked in the silver mines as had his father before him. He had joined the Western Federation of Miners two years after it was formed. Then he organized and became president of the local branch in Silver City, Utah, where he lived. Intelligent and forceful, he attracted the attention of the union's leaders almost immediately. In 1899, at the age of thirty, he was elected secretary-treasurer of the WFM.

Mary met Big Bill during the Colorado strike of 1904. Despite great differences in age and background—he was almost forty years younger than she, and had never set foot outside the United States—they had liked one another immediately.

They met again six months after the defeat in Colorado, when Haywood invited her to join with him and other radical labor leaders to discuss the creation of a new union. For after Colorado, Haywood had come to believe that individual unions were not, and never could be, strong enough to help the working people. It seemed to him that instead of separate unions for separate industries, all working people in America should join together in one big union. The American Federation of Labor, a "union of unions," already existed, but it accepted only skilled workers—machinists, carpenters, toolmakers—the "elite" of the working class. It didn't include farm workers, factory hands, lumberjacks, migrant workers, or laborers. And, Haywood thought, it was cautious and compromising, like its leader Samuel Gompers. It did

William "Big Bill" Haywood.

not wish to change the system. It only wished to get more of the benefits for its members.

Haywood wanted to create a union which would turn the country around. The way things were, he thought, America "belonged" to the landowners and the industrialists. He wanted it to "belong" to the workers. If all the workers joined together in one large union, eventually they could restructure society and do away with private ownership entirely. Then there would be no more distinction between "owners" and "workers." Everyone would be a worker, and the workers would own everything.

When Mary received Haywood's invitation to the conference, she accepted with interest. She thought he was original, honest, straightforward, and hard-hitting. And she had no difficulty accepting the new union's founding principle, worked out during the conference.

"The working class and the employing class have nothing in common," the statement read. "There can be no peace so long as hunger and want are found among millions of working people, and the few, who make up the employing class, have all the good things of life."

The conference was adjourned after three days, but the participants met again in June, 1905, when a general meeting was called. At this meeting there were hundreds of people representing various unions and workers' groups. There were also some people who did not represent any particular group—like Mary, Debs, and Lucy Parsons, wife of Haymarket martyr Albert Parsons. The entire group made a pilgrimage to the graves of the Haymarket martyrs before settling down to the business at hand. All voted to accept the basic ideas that had been discussed at the first meeting. The new union, the Industrial Workers of the

World, was born. Declaring its devotion to all workers, but especially to the unskilled people at the bottom, it was the most radical and militant union the United States had ever seen. "Now comes the IWW," Haywood boomed out in his deep, strong voice, "with the first bold and brotherly cry these ignorant masses have ever heard."

Mary admired Haywood and endorsed the ideals of the IWW, but she did not stay with the organization. Most of the men and women devoted to the IWW were, like Haywood himself, strong-willed, independent thinkers. As soon as the union was founded, personalities clashed, arguments broke out, and factions arose. Some members wanted to concentrate on political action. Others wanted to go out and organize workers into local branches. Some thought all members should be equal and that there should be no full-time leaders. Others thought strong central leadership was absolutely essential. The debates and discussions seemed endless.

Haywood had strong convictions about the way the IWW should be structured and how it should proceed. He was willing to work through the disagreements for the sake of the future. But Mary was impatient, as always, to get on with the work of the present. She was not a serious student of political theory or economic theory, the way many of the others were. She did not take sides in the disputes and soon turned her attention back to the conflicts and problems of the people. In later years, when the IWW waged high-spirited campaigns on both the west and the east coasts, Mary was involved in other conflicts with other groups of workers. So her presence at the founding conventions was her only real connection with the IWW.

But the convention had brought her close to Haywood. When, in June, he left Chicago to return to Colorado, they intended to

An early IWW poster.

keep in touch with each other. Six months later Governor Steunenberg was killed. And two months after that, Mary read in the newspaper that Haywood, along with Philip Moyer, president of the WFM, and George Pettibone, a business agent for the union, had been arrested for murder.

Idaho was basing its case against the unionists on the testimony of a man named Harry Orchard. He had confessed to planting the bomb which killed the governor, and to seventeen other murders in the course of the last year and a half. Orchard claimed that in all of them he had been acting on orders from Haywood and the "inner circle" of the WFM.

The state claimed to believe Harry Orchard's confession. Mary, the leaders of the WFM, the IWW, and virtually every other labor organization in the United States did not. But presenting a defense that would stand up in court would be difficult. Public support for the accused men would have to be high. A talented lawyer would have to be hired. Money would have to be raised.

For the next year and a half, while the men were in prison, Mary made a campaign tour for money and publicity that took her to almost every state in the nation. She said Haywood and the others had taken up "the battle for the oppressed" against a system which had "no soul and no love for humanity." As a result, their lives were on the line. The people must help them.

Other well-known people and influential organizations worked hard for the accused men, too. Eugene Debs declared that the working people of the country would rise up in armed revolt if the defendants were executed—and that he would encourage them to do so. Labor unions, especially of course the WFM and the IWW, turned their attention away from strikes and organizing drives and devoted all their energy to helping the prisoners. Even the American Federation of Labor threw its support wholeheartedly into the effort.

In January, 1907, the trial began. The case against Haywood was heard first. Spectators, including Mary and Debs and other prominent figures—as well as reporters from every major newspaper in the country—filled the gallery. Clarence Darrow had been hired as attorney for the defense. The most brilliant and the most famous trial lawyer in the nation, Darrow had his pick of cases. But he preferred to take up the defense of underdogs, people with the odds against them, especially those who did not have power or prestige or "friends in high places." He had defended unions and unionists before, including Eugene Debs in 1894, prompting Mary to call him "labor's great pleader." Now he appeared on behalf of Haywood, Moyer, and Pettibone.

Under Darrow's skillful cross-examination, Orchard's testimony fell apart. The claim that he had been "put up to" the murders by the unionists was not believable. If anything, it seemed that he had been "put up" by the mining companies—put up to blaming the unionists. Darrow's summation—his final speech to the jury—lasted for eleven hours. The jury was out for twenty hours. But when they returned, their verdict was "not guilty." After that, Moyer was quickly found innocent, and the case against George Pettibone was dropped without even being brought to trial. The men had spent eighteen months in prison. Now they were free.

Haywood went on a speaking tour for the IWW after the trial. Moyer and Pettibone focused on putting the WFM back together. Both unions had lost a great deal of ground during the imprisonment and trial of their leaders.

Mary, too, worked for the WFM, going first north, to the Michigan copper mines, and then south to Arizona, where the WFM was trying to rebuild its local branches. It was while she was there that she became involved in yet another strenuous defense. This time it was the Mexican revolutionaries whose cause she took up.

Mary had just returned to her hotel room in Douglas, Arizona, where she was holding a series of meetings, when the editor of the town's Spanish-language newspaper rushed in. He was so flustered and upset that it was a few minutes before Mary could make out what he was saying. At first it was only clear that "something" had happened to a man named Manuel Sarabia. Mary had met Sarabia that afternoon. She knew he had fought against the Mexican dictator, Porfirio Diaz, and had come to America for refuge. Under Mary's quiet questioning, the editor managed to tell the whole story.

He and Sarabia, an apprentice printer, had been at the newspaper office when "an official car" pulled up and two men came inside. They had seized Sarabia, forced him into the car, and driven off in the direction of the border.

"They took him to Mexico," the editor said. "Mother, what will we do?"

"Get all the facts you can," Mary said, standing up. "Get them as correct as you can and telegraph them to the governor. Telegraph to Washington. Don't waste a moment, because if you do they will murder him."

Though it was already close to midnight, Mary hurried out to set up a meeting for the next night. She wanted as many people as possible to know about the incident, and she wanted the Mexican government to know that Americans knew. It was Sarabia's only chance.

At the rally, Mary called the incident a "kidnaping" and said she was enraged at the idea of any "bloodthirsty pirate on a throne" reaching across the border and "stamping under his feet the Constitution of the United States." The kidnaping was a crime against all the people in the world who were struggling for freedom. They must make themselves heard. They must not let Sarabia be harmed.

When the rally was over, she urged all present to send telegrams of protest to every official they could think of—especially President Theodore Roosevelt. Hundreds of telegrams went out within the hour. "We got Teddy out of bed that night, I can tell you," Mary said, jubilant over the response.

Eight days later, a black car pulled up at the border and a young man, thin but smiling, stepped out and quietly crossed over to the American side. Manuel Sarabia had been freed.

A few months later, in October, three revolutionary leaders, fleeing from Diaz's troops, made their way across the border and regrouped in Los Angeles. They wanted to spread publicity about the Mexican revolution, and build support for the Mexican cause. Soon, however, they were arrested by American authorities. The grounds for the arrests were not clear. But, due to the efforts of Mary and other concerned individuals and groups, the arrests were given a great deal of space in American newspapers. So was Diaz's request, forwarded almost immediately, that they be returned to Mexico.

Mary traveled up and down the Pacific Coast to raise public opinion in support of the Mexicans. "They are patriots," she said, "like Garibaldi and George Washington—these Mexican men in jail, fighting against a bloodier tyrant than King George against whom we revolted." She hoped that "through the efforts we are making and the publicity we are giving them, they will not be turned over to Diaz to be murdered."

Several months later, the trial was held. The men were convicted of violating the "neutrality laws," which forbade people in America from planning or aiding political movements in other countries. But the other charges—among them murder and robbery, which Mary thought had been trumped up to begin with—were dropped. The men were sentenced to eighteen months in prison.

The fact that they were not sent back to Mexico made the trial a real victory, and Mary was pleased. Now she went to work for their release, and for their right to remain in the United States once they were out of prison. Speaking at conventions and meetings around the country, she raised money for an appeal and urged people to continue to put pressure on the government. "We have got to get those boys out of jail," she said. "We have got to let them live in this land; we have got to let them fight Mexico from here."

The men in prison wrote her this letter: "You are setting a noble example and teaching a lesson humanity will not forget. You, an old woman, are fighting with indomitable courage; you, an American, are devoting your life to free Mexican slaves. And they will be free in the near future, and they will learn to call you 'Mother.' "

The men had almost completed their sentences and were due to be sent back to Mexico upon their release, when Congress agreed to let the House Rules Committee investigate "the case of the Mexican refugees." Mary was one of the witnesses called to testify. She said that it was America's duty, as the "cradle of liberty," to help people in other countries who were fighting for their freedom. Instead of cooperating with dictators like Diaz, the United States should help the people who were trying to overthrow him. "In the name of our own revolutionary heroes," Mary told the committee, "I beg that this body will protect these Mexican men from the tyranny and oppression of that bloody tyrant Diaz."

The hearings lasted for five days. When they were over, the men were released and invited to remain in the United States for as long as they wished.

Soon there was more news out of Mexico. Diaz's dictatorship had been overthrown. One of the first things the new Mexican government did was to give Mexican workers a right Diaz had denied them—the right to organize and form unions. Then it invited Mary, along with an official from the UMW and one from the WFM, to come to Mexico and join the celebration. Crowds cheered for them all, but it was clear that Mary was the one they loved. The people sang songs to her and applauded wildly whenever she appeared. By the time she left Mexico, she could count the people there among her admiring, warm-hearted supporters. Before very long, the tables would be turned, and Mary would be in prison. When that happened, her new friends would do everything they could to help.

೭ TWELVE ೨

WEST VIRGINIA AGAIN

The spring of 1912 found Mary in the West, with railroad workers who had struck against the Pacific Northwest Railroad. In April, she was in Milwaukee, helping women workers in a bottling plant. In May, she was in Montana, where copper miners were on strike. In June, she moved on to Denver to rest and visit with friends.

But then Mary heard the news coming out of West Virginia. "I tied up all my possessions in a black shawl," she said, "—I like traveling light—and went immediately."

The news out of West Virginia was war—pitched battles between company guards and miners. The place was the Kanawha Valley, the very area in which Mary had worked eight years earlier. "I had helped the miners organize that district in 1904," she said, "and now the battle had to be fought all over again."

The Kanawha Valley was divided in half by a high, sharp ridge which ran down the center. On one side of the ridge was Cabin Creek, and the Cabin Creek Mining Company. On the other side, eight miles away, was Paint Creek and the Paint Creek Mining Company. Local branches of the UMW had been established in both parts of the valley in 1904, when Mary left the area. But the local at Cabin Creek had been destroyed two years later, and armed guards had been hired to make sure that organizers did not return. The local at Paint Creek, on the other side of the valley, had held on—until the spring of 1912. Then the contract between the miners and the owners expired and the owners refused to sign another. The miners called a strike. The UMW sent in organizers, and the companies brought in armed guards. Within days, the fighting began.

Mary arrived in Charleston, the capital of West Virginia, in mid-July. Addressing a group of workers on the Charleston levee, she blamed the governor for the fighting in the valley. He had the authority to stop it, she said. He could order the companies to call off their guards. He could ban the Baldwin-Felts Detective Agency, which supplied the companies with gunmen, from the state altogether. But he hung back and allowed the companies to do whatever they wished. Before a thousand people, Mary called the governor a "goddamned dirty coward." "I warn this little governor," she went on, "that unless he rids Paint Creek and Cabin Creek of these . . . mine-guard thugs, there is going to be one hell of a lot of bloodletting in these hills."

On the levee with Mary that night was a man named Ralph Chapin, a writer, an IWW organizer, and a sharp observer. This is how he described the scene.

She might have been any coal miner's wife ablaze with righteous fury when her brood was in danger. Her voice shrilled as she shook her fist at the coal operators, the mine guards. . . . She prayed and cursed and pleaded, raising her clenched and trembling hands, asking heaven to bear witness. She wore long, very full skirts and a black shawl and her tiny bonnet bobbed up and down as she harangued the crowd. The miners loved it and laughed, cheered, hooted, and even cried as she spoke to them.

Toward the end of her speech, Mary paused to climb onto a wagon that was nearby. "I want to see if the guards are here," she said, peering over the heads of the people as they cheered her. Then, in a quieter voice, she concluded. "We are not going to surrender," she said. "We are going to do business with the bloodhounds."

Again and again in the days that followed, Mary was warned not to enter the Creek district itself. But every day found her closer to the scene of the fighting. On August 4, she held a meeting in Montgomery, fifteen miles from the mouth of Cabin Creek. The next day she was on her way to Paint Creek Junction.

The train, Mary recalled, "wound in and out among the mountains, dotted here and there with the desolate little cabins of miners." At Paint Creek Junction, where Mary climbed off, "there were a lot of gunmen, armed to the teeth, lolling about. Everything was still and no one would know of the bloody war that was raging in those silent hills, except for the sight of those guns and the strange, terrified look on everyone's face." Mary stood for a moment, "looking up at the everlasting hills." Then she walked through the little town, staring at and being stared at by the guards. She visited with the families she knew and introduced herself to people she had not met before.

The companies, Mary learned, had built a camp for their guards at Mucklow, five miles up Paint Creek. Overlooking the river, a machine gun in plain view, the camp was a grim fortress. Every morning, guards marched out in groups of two and three. Everywhere, Mary saw signs of their brutality, evidence that the companies were determined to end the strike by a sheer show of force. Men, women, and children had been threatened and beaten by the guards. One child, covered with bruises, cried that his father had been driven away, and the family didn't know where he was. "They threw my mama and all the kids out of the house," he said, "and they beat my mama and they beat me." The boy pulled open his shirt to show Mary his shoulders. They were black and blue. Although on other occasions Mary spoke against violence, claiming that "violence only produces more violence," she would soon be urging the miners of Paint Creek to protect themselves— with guns if need be. "If you haven't got good guns," she said to one group, "buy them."

After a few days with the miners in Paint Creek, Mary realized that she must reach the miners of Cabin Creek and get them to join the strike. But how? The men called Cabin Creek "Ole Russia" and explained that the entire hollow—seventeen miles long—was heavily guarded.

There was one possibility, Mary learned from the Paint Creek miners. There was a city in the Cabin Creek district which was "free." Eskdale, they said, was a town which had been settled before the arrival of the coal companies. It was incorporated, and the companies had no authority there. Eskdale, then, was a safe haven, a place where a meeting could be held. Mary decided to speak there the evening of August 6.

Although Mary was not officially working for the UMW, she was in close contact with the organizers who were. They agreed that Cabin Creek had to be "brought out," and one of them offered to go with her to Eskdale. But Mary thought it would be better if she went alone. "You represent the national office," she said. "I don't. If anything happens and you are there, the operators can blame the union. . . . I go as a private citizen. All they can do to me is put me in jail."

Mary took the train to Eskdale and that night she spoke to a small gathering of Cabin Creek miners. "You have come over the mountains, twelve, sixteen miles. Your clothes are thin . . . your wives and little ones are cold and hungry." Mary told them that their "goodness and patience" had "cried out to a deaf world." Now they must stop being patient. They must join their brothers in Paint Creek; they must join the union once more, and strike.

First one man, then another, then all of them stepped forward and took the union pledge. Mary told them that she would notify union headquarters and that the men should go back home and go to work as usual. "Say nothing about being a union man," she advised them. "Put on your overalls, take your dinner buckets, go to work in the mines." Once there, they should talk to the other miners and get them to come out for the union too.

The men were willing, but they didn't get the chance to spread the word. For the next day, when they reported for work, they were all fired. Company spies had been at the meeting and had taken down the names of everyone there. This was a common company tactic, designed to frighten workers from attending

"MOTHER" JONES TALKS TO MINERS ON CABIN CREEK, AND STRIKE WILL FOLLOW

OBNOXIOUS GUARDS FROM PAINT CREEK WERE TRANSFERRED TO CABIN CREEK—TROUBLE THERE SO ON FOLLOWED—BOOMER TROUBLES ARE PRACTICALLY SETTLED—6,000 MEN ARE STILL ON STRIKE

CHARLESTON, August 11.—Growing out of the strike of coal miners on Paint creek, which has been on since the middle of last April, is an organized movement having for its purpose the organization of all coal miners in West Virginia for a general strike. Definite information to this effect has been received by State officials though the operators in fields now without apparent strike troubles declare it unfounded, while the officials of the union miners only partially admit it.

With the exception of a part of the Knawha field and the northern Panhandle the miners of the state are not known members of the union. Where the miners are organized muchtrouble was experienced in agreeing upon a new scale when the old agree-ment expired April first. Agreements were finally reached at practically all the mines except Paint creek, in the Kanawha field, where about one-fifthof the full force is now working. The entire state militia, with the exception of two companies which are on duty at Peytona and Sterling, is on duty on Paint creek. The Peytona and Sterling troubles have been settled and tomorrow the militia there will return home, one company to Charleston and the other to Kingwood.

Taking advantage of the Paint Creek situation the organizers for the United Mine Workers of America have been attempting to effect an organization wherever coal is mined in the state. How far they have succeeded is kept from the public. It is definitely known, however, that they have gone far enough to threaten a State-wide strike, whether the miners really have joined the union or not. The operators, generally, in the state are uneasy though they declare there is nochance of such a strike. There is apparent a feeling of unrest among theminers, notwithstanding in many sections they are making more money thanever before.

The demand of the miners on Paint creek, if conceded, would give them an increase of from two to two and one-half cents per ton. About fifteen hundred miners are on strike there but, according to the strikers themselves, their main grievance now is the treatment received by them at the

A 1912 newspaper account of Mary's activities in Cabin Creek.

union meetings. But the Cabin Creek miners had already been pushed too far. The presence of an organizer in their district had given them hope—and spirit. Attendance at the next meeting Mary held in Eskdale was greater than that at the first. Cabin Creek had begun to move.

The mine operators denied that their workers had any legitimate grievances. Instead, they claimed that their workers had been "entirely contented" with the way things were—until the organizers came and stirred them up. "Through distortion of fact," one company report said, "the union organizers so aroused the passions of the miners that men who were usually level-headed threw all self-restraint to the winds and followed these leaders with the blind faith of children." One manager described Mary to his supervisor as "The Old Hag," saying "we must keep characters like that from going near the mines."

The second Eskdale meeting was held on the thirteenth of August. When it was over, a group of miners came forward to introduce themselves to Mary. They were from the Red Warrior mining camp, in the Cabin Creek district about fifteen miles north of Eskdale. There were many other miners there, but they were too frightened to come to town. Would Mary come to the camp and speak there? They had brought a buggy for her to ride in. They would go with her in case she ran into trouble on the road.

Mary agreed. She traveled along the dry creek bed, since that was the only "road" not owned by the company and she could not be arrested for trespassing. The men walked along the railroad tracks which paralleled the creek.

"As we were bumping along," Mary wrote, "I heard a scream. I looked up at the tracks along which the miners were walking. I saw the men running. . . . I jumped out of the buggy and started to run to the tracks. 'Stand still!' I called. 'Stand where you are. I'm coming!' "

What Mary saw when she reached the tracks was a contingent of company guards, perhaps fifty altogether, milling around beside a machine gun. "I walked up to the gunmen," she recalled, "and put my hand over the muzzle of the gun."

"Take your hand off that gun!" one of the guards yelled.

"Young man," Mary said, "I want to tell you that if you shoot one bullet out of this gun at those men, if you touch one of my white hairs, that creek will run with blood. . . . Up there in the mountains," she continued, pointing at the dark hills all around, "I have five hundred miners. They are marching armed to the meeting I am going to address. If you start the shooting, they will finish the game."

The guards did not say anything after that, and the group continued on its way. Of course, there were no armed miners in the hills. "Just jackrabbits, perhaps," Mary said later. "But I realized that we were up against it, and something had to be done. . . . so I pulled the dramatic stuff on those thugs."

The next week, Mary went to Wineberg, another mining camp in the Cabin Creek district. Mary was walking along the train tracks with a newspaper reporter from Baltimore when she was again stopped by gunmen. They ordered her and the reporter out of the district—unless they wished to walk in the creek bed, and on that day the water was high.

"You don't mean to say you are going to make that old lady walk that creek in that ice-cold water, do you?" the reporter asked.

"It's too damn good for her," the guard said, laughing. "She won't walk it."

"Oh, won't I?" Mary said. And she took off her shoes, rolled up her skirt, and waded into the creek.

Mary got to Wineberg and held the meeting—in the creek.

The struggle continued. As Mary and the other organizers recruited more miners into the union, the brutality of the company guards increased. Mary found no words to comfort the pregnant woman beaten by guards, her unborn child kicked dead. She spoke to a young boy who "sobbed out his sorrows, sorrows no little child should ever witness." The miners brought out their weapons, "as did the early settlers," Mary wrote, "to protect themselves against the attacks of wild Indians." The Creek district was at war. Still, the governor did not intervene.

Mary thought they should put more pressure on the state government. In cooperation with the union, she planned a march to the state capital. At the end of August hundreds of miners made their way to Charleston, some by train, some by wagon, and some by foot. They milled through the streets carrying banners and flags. One of the banners pictured Governor Glassock as Nero, the ancient emperor of Rome, who was supposed to have played his fiddle while his city burned to the ground. Wasn't Governor Glassock entertaining himself while his state was plunging toward civil war?

The miners gathered on the steps of the capitol building. Three speakers preceded Mary, but she was the main attraction. First she demanded that the governor prohibit the use of mine guards. Then she spoke directly to the miners. "I know your aching backs," she said. "I know your swimming heads. I know your little children suffer." Looking out over the faces on the capitol steps, she told the people that they would win their struggle. "We have fought together, we have marched together, we have hungered together. But I can see victory in the heavens for you."

She spoke scornfully of the mine owners, accusing them of starving their workers so they could take home huge profits. About their wives she said: "They wear five dollars' worth of paint on their faces and have toothbrushes for their dogs, and they say, 'Oh, them horrible miners,' and 'Oh, that horrible old Mother Jones, that horrible old woman.' " The crowd cheered and applauded, and Mary waited a moment before she continued. "I am horrible, I admit," she finally said, "and I want you to be horrible to those blood-sucking pirates."

Toward the end of her speech Mary interrupted herself to tell the miners to "be good" and not to drink "more than one glass of beer." But in case someone could not afford even that, she asked the miners to "pass the hat around."

One old man walked up to her and said, "Here is ten dollars. Shake hands with me, an old union miner. ... If I don't have enough to pay my railroad fare, I will walk. I don't care if this was the last cent I had, I will give it to Mother and go and get more."

Governor Glassock did not respond to Mary's demand that he order the mine guards out of the Creek district. He did not respond to the demonstration at all. The miners left for their homes, and before they did, they bought guns.

In the Kanawha Valley, the mines were still operating, but at a very slow rate. They were worked by a skeleton crew of miners who had not joined the strike. It had been on for almost three months now, but the owners were still determined not to yield to the union. Noting with satisfaction the governor's refusal to listen to the strikers' appeal in Charleston, the owners stepped up their effort to drive the strikers and the organizers away. They had given up their hope of getting the men back on the job, and now they wanted to bring in strikebreakers, get the mines operating normally again, and be rid of the union once and for all. Feelings grew still more bitter as the violence on both sides increased. In one incident, company guards fired on the strikers' tent colony at Holly Grove. In another, a group of miners shot at the guards at their camp at Mucklow. The companies brought in still more heavy equipment, including two additional machine guns. By the middle of September, miners from outside the valley were coming in to help the strikers. By the end of the month, approximately 2,000 men were massed and preparing for battle.

Now Governor Glassock came to the Kanawha Valley. He concluded that a "state of war" existed and declared martial law; 1,200 militiamen were brought in and stationed at the creeks. They confiscated weapons by the hundreds, including rifles, pistols, blackjacks, daggers, bayonets, and brass knuckles. Many of the miners did not turn over all their weapons but hid them in the woods for the time when they would be needed again. The fact that the company's machine guns remained in place, unchallenged by the militia, was not lost on them.

The troops remained until late in October and things were quiet for as long as they were there. But the order to withdraw created a situation which was far worse than that which had existed before. Dismissed from active duty on behalf of the state, hundreds of soldiers were offered jobs with the mining companies—as private guards. Most of them accepted. With a full force of well-trained troops at their disposal, the companies could do as they pleased. Within the week, they were bringing in large groups of strikebreakers from New York and Chicago. The strikebreakers were delivered to the Creek district on special trains, guarded on their way to the mines in the morning and on their way to their houses in the evening.

The guards claimed to be protecting them from possible attack by the strikers. But it was soon clear that they also wanted to prevent the strikebreakers from leaving. The men had not been told what was happening in West Virginia when they had been hired. Once they understood, many of them wanted to leave—and were stopped from doing so by the guards.

A peculiar situation developed. As strangers in the valley, the strikebreakers did not know the routes out. With the roads and passes blocked, they were trapped. But the strikers had lived in the valley all of their lives; they could find their way out without ever going near a road. So it came about that from time to time a union man would slip out of his tent at night to lead a group of strikebreakers through the mountains, out of the hollow and into free territory. Stories of these "freedom raids" are told in the mountains of West Virginia to this day.

On the whole, however, in spite of the "desertions," the companies were gaining and the strikers losing. The mines were operating, and the guards were in complete control.

Mary determined to "open" the valley—to publicize what was happening, in order to persuade the federal government to step in. Borrowing money, she arranged a speaking tour, and went first to Wheeling, West Virginia, then Cincinnati, Columbus, Cleveland, and finally Washington, D.C. She visited the members of Congress in their offices and in their homes, urging them to send an investigating committee to the Kanawha Valley. A few politicians refused to see her; others were skeptical. But some were shocked and upset by what she told them and promised to

Mary with Terence Powderly (center) *and William B. Wilson, first Secretary of Labor.*

look into the situation. William B. Wilson, in the newly created position of Secretary of Labor, had been a miner himself once and an officer in the UMW. He had worked with Mary years before in Pennsylvania. He knew that what she was saying was true, and promised to do everything in his power to get an investigation started. Mary also spoke in the Washington Armory, and described the battle to the public at large.

By the time Mary returned to West Virginia, martial law was in effect once again. The companies, perhaps to rid the Creek district of strikers once and for all, had sent an armored train fitted out with machine guns through the valley. The guards on board had fired on the strikers' tent colony at Holly Grove, killing five people and wounding several others. In return, the miners had attacked the guard camp at Mucklow. Two companies of militia were ordered back to the area. Hundreds of strikers were arrested, but no action was taken against the companies.

When Mary arrived, the miners asked her to go to the state capital to plead for them. She selected a committee of thirty-four men to accompany her, and together they boarded the train for Charleston. But rumors reached the capital before they did. The story going around was that Mary, with "an army of 3,500," was on her way to kill the governor and blow up the capitol building.

The group got off the train, unaware of the rumors that had preceded them; Mary was seized, thrown into a waiting auto-mobile, and driven away. At the railroad depot on the other side of town, she was placed aboard a special train and taken to military headquarters in Pratt, West Virginia, in the strike zone. She was charged with stealing a machine gun, attempting to blow up a train with dynamite, and conspiracy to commit murder—a charge for which the penalty was death. She was placed in military confinement in the guardhouse.

Mary's arrest and imprisonment accomplished what she had long been trying for: it brought massive publicity to the West Virginia strike. Questions and protests from all over the country came pouring into the governor's office. Reporters appeared at Pratt demanding that they be allowed to speak to Mary. What proof did the government have against her? How long would it be before a trial? Why was she being subjected to a military tribunal? Wasn't she going to have a trial by jury? What was going on in West Virginia anyway?

The reporters were not allowed to see Mary. But she managed to give them a statement as she was being led up the steps to the courtroom.

"I am eighty years old," she said, "and I haven't long to live anyhow. Since I have to die, I would rather die for the cause to which I have given so much of my life. My death would call the attention of the whole United States to conditions in West Virginia. It would be worthwhile for that reason." Then, looking at the guards standing uneasily beside the huge courthouse doors, she added, "I fear, though, that I shall not be executed."

In the courtroom, Mary refused to enter a plea. She argued that the military court had no right to try her, since she was a civilian arrested in a civilian zone. The UMW appealed her case, asking that it be transferred to the civil system. So Mary was ordered back in confinement until the higher courts could hand down a decision.

After twenty-two days, it was in: the UMW's appeal was turned down. Mary would face a military tribunal.

"My dear friend," Mary wrote to Terence Powderly on the day before the trial began, "You no doubt have heard of my arrest by the hounds of capital pirates. They have me in close confinement. There are 2 military guarding me day and night. No one is allowed to speak to me. . . . Tomorrow at 10 o'clock we will be taken before the military court . . . God spare me the heart to fight them. Love to my dear Emma. Tell her not to worry. I'll fight the pirates."

The trial began at 9:00 A.M. It was over before noon. The verdict was determined that afternoon but was not announced. Mary was kept in her quarters.

At just this time, a new governor was elected in West Virginia, thirty-seven-year-old Henry D. Hatfield. He was a physician, and although elected with the support of mine owners, he tried to find out for himself what the situation in the strike zone was like. He was informed of the verdict of the military court, but he kept it secret while he visited the valley. He inspected one of the miners' tent colonies, and then he went to the military encampment at Pratt. There he saw Mary. This is his description:

> I noticed a soldier marching to and fro in front of a little cabin on the banks of the Kanawha River. I told the soldier who I was and inquired what responsibility he had there. He told me Mother Jones was being guarded in this little shack and when I entered I found her lying on a straw tick on the floor, carrying a temperature of 104, very rapid respiration, and a constant cough. She had pneumonia.

Hatfield had Mary taken to Charleston where she was treated by a doctor. When she was strong enough, she was sent back to Pratt and placed in solitary confinement again.

The governor did not want news of Mary's illness to reach the press, but word leaked out when Mrs. Fremont Older, a well-known magazine writer, arrived at the camp. She was not allowed to see Mary, but with the instincts of a private detective, she got the story, wrote it for *Collier's Magazine,* and added her voice to the many people who were now pressuring members of Congress to order an investigation.

It was Senator Kern of Indiana who finally brought the issue to the floor of the Senate. Congress must send a commission to West Virginia, he said, for a "reign of terror" existed there. To prove his point, Senator Kern cited Mary's imprisonment.

Senator Goff of West Virginia protested. Mother Jones was not in prison at all, he said, but was only being "detained in a very pleasant boarding house." How did he know this? The governor himself had told him so, the Senator explained.

When Senator Goff sat down, Senator Kern rose, reached into his pocket, and slowly took out a piece of paper. It was a telegram, written by Mary and smuggled out of the military camp by a sympathetic soldier. Senator Kern read it out loud to a hushed audience.

From out the military prison walls in Pratt, West Virginia, where I have been forced to pass my 83rd milestone of life, I plead with you for the honor of this nation. I send you groans and tears and heartaches of men, women, and children as I have heard them in this state, and beg you to force an investigation. Children yet unborn will rise and bless you.

The debate continued, but the life had gone out of it. Senator Goff maintained that the mine owners deserved the protection of the state because they had "conquered the wilderness." And of

Mary, he said: "Good and grand and a friend of the miners she may be—but she certainly has been inciting riot and urging insurrection."

The events Senator Kern had described, however, persuaded almost everyone that something was very wrong in the state of West Virginia. By the end of the week, over Senator Goff's protests that things were "as they should be," a special congressional committee was on its way to the Kanawha Valley.

Governor Hatfield, under greater pressure now than ever before, took "the scandal of Kanawha Valley" into his own hands. He brought the companies to the conference table, forced them to recognize the union, and imposed what came to be called "the Hatfield Agreement." Many of the things for which the union had been fighting were granted: a nine-hour work day, the right to organize, the right to shop at other than the company store.

Governor Hatfield also guaranteed the right of citizens to be tried by civil not military courts, and he dismissed the sentences which the military courts had passed. It was then learned that Mary, eighty-three years old, had been sentenced to twenty years in prison. At the end of May, after almost three months in solitary confinement, she was released.

The world considered Mary the most heroic figure in the bitter struggle, but she paid tribute to the miners themselves. "More hungry, more cold, more starving, more ragged than Washington's army that fought against tyranny were the miners of the Kanawha Mountains. And just as grim. Just as heroic."

THIRTEEN

COLORADO: THE LAST TIME

When Mary left West Virginia, in the spring of 1913, she was eighty-three years old. One might have thought it was time to slow down, find a comfortable place to live, and get out of the line of fire. Terence Powderly and his wife, Emma, had invited Mary to make her home with them years before. They lived in a Washington suburb, and they had an extra room specifically reserved for friends and fellow-travelers in the labor movement. They told Mary that they would be happy to have her there permanently.

But Mary's health, her stamina and energy, and her interests were too strong for retirement. She stayed with the Powderlys for most of the summer, but by the end of August she was on a speaking tour in southwest Texas commemorating Labor Day. Then she received word from the UMW that trouble was brewing once again in Colorado. If she could go there, the union could use her help.

The UMW had returned to southern Colorado in 1907. John Lawson, a member of the executive board, had gone there to rebuild what was left of the union after the 1903 defeat. But he could not make any headway. The companies ruled the area with an iron hand.

Lawson and some fellow-organizers had moved north a few years later. There, the companies which had already accepted the union refused to negotiate a new contract. In 1910, the miners struck, and the southern companies urged the northern companies not to settle, but to crush the union as they themselves had done. Soon armed guards arrived in the area, and local judges, under pressure from the companies, began to issue injunctions against union activities. They forbade meetings, picket lines, speeches, and demonstrations.

The strikers were still out when the UMW held its annual convention in 1911. Much of the talk was about Colorado. Organizers who knew the state tried to persuade John White, elected president of the UMWA when John Mitchell resigned, to commit the union to a southern organizing drive. The UMW had abandoned the south in 1903, over the opposition of the organizers there, especially, of course, Mary. It had settled for the gains that were made in the north. But now those gains had been wiped out, and it was time to look anew at the entire Colorado field. Neither section could win a real victory alone, the organizers claimed. Neither would be safe until they were both unionized. Mary was one of those who made an impassioned appeal. "You have got to call a strike in the southern field and lick the Colorado Fuel and Iron Company out of its boots," she said. "You cannot win the northern field until you take a hand in the south . . . I am for making a fight on the whole bunch. If you don't want to do it alone, I will go there and take a hand in it and give them hell."

Slowly and cautiously, the union made its way into the tangled and dangerous southern field. A dozen organizers were sent in the spring of 1912. A union office was reopened in Trinidad in the fall. Then, in the spring of 1913, the UMW announced the beginning of an all-out southern drive. By the summer, experienced organizers who knew the territory, who knew both the miners and the opposition they faced, were dispatched to the Trinidad area. President White contacted Mary in Texas and she made plans to come immediately. It would be the toughest strike in which she had ever engaged.

Mary arrived in Trinidad on the fifteenth of September. Hatred and fear seemed to hang in the air. She had no sooner gotten off the train than she received an anonymous note telling her to get out of the area, and stay out. "They are sending me all sorts of threats here," she wrote to the Powderlys in Washington. "They have my skull drawn and two cross sticks beneath my jaw to tell me that if I do not quit they are going to get me."

Mary was not frightened away by threatening letters. Meeting with miners in and around Trinidad, her speeches were tough and fiery. "I hope there is no war in Trinidad," she said just after she arrived, "for it will cause suffering, but if the war has to be made that the boys in the mines may have their rights—let it come!"

Living conditions for the miners had hardly changed since Mary toured their settlements in 1903. The company houses, according to one of the company's own investigators, were among "the most repulsive-looking rat-holes to be found anywhere in America." Some of them were "hovels, shacks and dugouts unfit for the habitation of human beings . . . little removed from the pig-sty make of dwellings." Filth and crowding were responsible for outbreaks of typhoid fever yearly—151 cases in 1911 alone. And the mines themselves were terribly dangerous. Scores of workers were killed every year in accidents that could have been prevented had the companies taken proper precautions. It was cheaper to replace a worker killed in a cave-in than to keep the mines propped so that a cave-in would not happen. There seemed to be an unlimited supply of workers—most of them immigrants— and if one left, or was injured, or killed, there were others to take his place.

"Rise up and strike!" Mary said at a mass meeting in the Trinidad Opera House. "If it is slavery or strike, I say strike until the last one of you drop into your graves. Strike and stay with it as we did in West Virginia!"

There was loud applause for the miners who had just gone through an awful struggle, and for Mary herself, who had gone through it with them. Sensing this, Mary pledged to remain with the Colorado miners. "We are going to stay here in southern Colorado," she said, "until the banner of industrial freedom floats over every coal mine. We are going to stand together and never surrender."

While the organizers were in the field, the UMW sent several requests to the companies, asking for a conference. The union's letters went unanswered, and union members, at a statewide meeting, voted to strike.

On September 23, the strike began. On that day too, there was a blizzard. Ten thousand miners, over 80 percent of all the miners in the south, trudged through the snow and sleet from the company houses to the tents that had been prepared beforehand.

There were twelve tent colonies in all, the biggest one near a town called Ludlow. The dangers the families faced were clear even as they filed silently along the roads.

Rockefeller's Colorado Fuel and Iron Company, still the most powerful in the southern part of the state, had hired an army of guards in preparation for the strike. Now the guards stood, rifles in hand, hurrying the strikers off company property. The old, the sick, women who were pregnant, children who wanted to run back for a last look were pushed and shoved along the road. Many of

Soldiers of the Colorado National Guard outside the Ludlow Saloon.

the guards had been made deputy sheriffs—while continuing to be employed and paid by the CFI. That was against the law. The men should have given up their positions with the companies—or not been deputized. The U.S. Commission on Industrial Relations, which later investigated the strike, concluded that "many guards deputized in this illegal fashion and paid by the CFI were men of the lowest and most vicious character."

Colorado miners who have armed themselves.

The Colorado authorities claimed that they deputized these men so that they might help to "keep the peace." But with the first day of the strike came the murder of the first unionists, and it was clear to everyone what the guards were there for.

Heavy ammunition had been purchased by the CFI, including some of the same machine guns that had been used against the strikers in West Virginia. The CFI also designed and had built an armored car, which the guards nicknamed "The Death Special." It was fitted out with a machine gun capable of shooting 400 times a minute. During the first week of the strike, the car, manned by five deputies, went to a strikers' tent colony near the town of Forbes. A writer from *Harper's Weekly* was there. This is his report of what happened.

> [The car] stopped just a short distance from the Camp and one of the men took a white handkerchief, put it on the end of a stick and using it as a flag of truce approached the group of strikers. As he came up he asked if they were Union men, and receiving their reply in the affirmative, he threw down the flag, jumped to one side and said "Look out for yourselves." At that the machine gun cut loose on the crowd. One hundred and forty-seven bullets were put through one tent; a boy 15 years old was shot 9 times in the legs; one miner was killed, shot through the forehead. This was but one of a series of incidents.

The miners armed themselves with whatever rifles and shotguns they could obtain. But they were in no position to "fight fire with fire" in an out-and-out war against the companies.

The union made request after request to company officials,

asking for no more than a chance to negotiate. But their requests went unanswered.

Under pressure from people all around the state, the governor of Colorado, Elias Ammons, came to Trinidad to investigate. Mary led a parade of women and children to the hotel where he was staying, but he refused to see them. However, after touring the roads and camps, he called up the state militia.

Many miners felt that the militia would protect them. But Mary was not reassured. If she had learned anything in West Virginia, it was that the safety of "her boys" could not be entrusted to the state militia. Almost immediately, she went to Washington. She wanted the federal government on the scene. She wanted Congress to send an investigating committee to Colorado, to take a hand in the situation there.

Although several important members of Congress took an interest in the Colorado strike and promised to do whatever they could to help, the situation grew worse day by day. In a reversal of what had happened in West Virginia, where the coal companies had hired soldiers as private guards, in Colorado, company guards were being recruited into the militia. The result was the same. The militia became a company army. Soldiers broke up legal meetings of strikers, harassed their children, threatened and attacked the miners. Brigadier General John Chase, commander of the militia, rode around in a Colorado Fuel and Iron Company car. He made no attempt to appear impartial.

Mary was alarmed, so alarmed that only two days after she returned from Washington, she was off to Denver to see what she could do about the state militia. Speaking at a meeting of the State Labor Convention, she explained what had become of the troops and their commander in the southern field, and she asked the delegates to help her get them out. Some of the delegates were women, and Mary urged them not to hold back for fear of "public opinion." They could "bring Governor Ammons to time double quick," she told them, and they mustn't be concerned about the criticism they would receive, though they were sure to be condemned as "unladylike." "A lady," Mary said, "is a female whose skull is adorned with four feet of feathers. A woman is one whose skull is full of gray matter—studying the conditions beneath the surface."

Would all the delegates march with her to the capitol building to demand that Ammons take some action? Two thousand unionists stood up to follow Mary out of the hall and down the street to the governor's office. He heard them out, but afterwards he claimed he had no proof that what they had said was true. If they could produce a report, including names and places, he said, he would reconsider.

Mary thought Governor Ammons was stalling. But the state convention was willing to send a committee down, on the chance that it would do some good. Meanwhile, Mary returned to Trinidad.

The state militia had begun to bring in strikebreakers for the companies, something Governor Ammons had originally ordered them not to do. The companies were recruiting people in Mexico, massing them in El Paso, Texas, and having the militia escort them to the Colorado mines. The strikebreakers "were brought into the strike territory without knowing the conditions, promised enormous wages and easy work," Mary said. And once they were there, the militia did not allow them to leave.

Mary went to El Paso, "to give the facts of the Colorado strike to the Mexicans." She held meetings. She attended Mexican gatherings. She spoke wherever and whenever she could, in order to "get the story over the border." "I did everything in my power," she said, "to prevent strikebreakers from coming into the Colorado mines."

Back in Trinidad, General Chase was doing everything in his power to prevent Mary from returning. On December 17, he announced that if she did come back, she would be arrested. "I am not going to give her a chance to make any more speeches here," the general said. "She is dangerous because she inflames the minds of the strikers. She will be jailed immediately if she comes to Trinidad."

Mary's response to his announcement was quoted in newspapers throughout the Southwest. "Tell General Chase that Mother Jones is going to Trinidad in a day or two and that he'd better play his strongest cards—the militia's guns—against her. He had better go back to his mother and get a nursing bottle. He'll be better there than making war on an eighty-three-year-old woman."

Mary was true to her word. When she was finished in El Paso, she returned to Trinidad. General Chase was true to his word, too. When she stepped off the train, she was arrested and taken by military escort to a train bound for Denver. As the soldiers led her away, Mary called out that she would return "when Colorado is made part of the United States."

The train carrying Mary pulled into Walsenburg Station, the first stop north of Trinidad, just at dusk. A group of miners was waiting on the platform. They began to wave to Mary as soon as the train came into sight. Then they sang a song that could be heard in camps throughout the state, "The Union Forever."

"They sang at the tops of their lungs," Mary wrote, "til the silent old mountains seemed to prick up their ears."

There were guards at the station too. Some of them were swinging their guns about, hoping to draw the miners into a fight.

When the train stopped, some of the miners came on board and offered to stay with Mary. One wanted to give her his coat. Mary thanked them, and told them not to worry. She said she would be fine. And she would be back.

In Denver, Mary was put off the train. Not the least shaken or frightened by the militia, she spoke the next night at a meeting of the Denver Trades and Labor Assembly. "I serve notice on the governor that this state doesn't belong to him," she said, "it belongs to the nation and I own a share of stock in it. Ammons or Chase, either one can shoot me, but I will talk from the grave."

Mary remained "in exile" from the strike zone for eight days—from the fourth of January, when the militia deposited her in Denver, until the twelfth. During that time, she met with UMW officials and purchased supplies for the miners—including $500 worth of shoes for the men and their families. Perhaps this purchase was the inspiration behind a story published in a coal company bulletin. The story has enough detail to suggest that some research went into it. It charged that the union was making a profit from the strike, and singled out Mary as an example of an organizer who was being "very well paid" for her work. Her salary for the past nine weeks, the article claimed, had been $2,668.62—which would have made Mary the best-paid organizer in America. Actually, Mary did receive $2,668.62 from the UMW—for the entire year. And of that, only $940 was salary. The remaining $1,728 was for expenses—including the $500 used in purchasing the shoes. Mary could easily have accounted for the rest of the expense money—she made many purchases on behalf of the strikers—but she did not bother to answer the charges company publications made against her.

On January 12, she set out for Trinidad again. Avoiding the Denver train station, where detectives were posted, she made her way into the yard where the trains were prepared for the next run. It was closed to the public, and only the railroad workers themselves ever went there. Mary knew they were sympathetic with the miners, and she soon found a brakeman who showed her to the train which was scheduled to depart for Trinidad that after-noon. When it pulled out, she was resting comfortably in a berth, with no one but the conductor aware she was on board.

Early the next morning, during a short stop just north of Trinidad, Mary got off and walked into town, thus avoiding the detectives at the Trinidad station. But by mid-afternoon, the militia knew she was back. This time, General Chase, calling her a "contentious witch," had her arrested and placed under military confinement in the Mt. San Rafael Hospital on the outskirts of the city. The hospital was run by the Sisters of Charity, but outside Mary's room military guards kept a twenty-four-hour watch.

Word of her arrest and confinement spread quickly, and just as quickly, demonstrations and protests flared up. What were the grounds for her confinement? strikers and the general public de-manded to know. She had not been charged with a crime. No trial had been held, nor was one scheduled.

General Chase and Governor Ammons barely responded to the protests, which further infuriated the people. UMW lawyers filed a petition to have her released, pending a hearing. But the petition was denied. A group of miners, almost a thousand strong, wired the governor that they would free Mary by force if he did not order her release. A group of women marched through Trinidad's main streets waving banners that said "God Bless Mother Jones," and "We're for Mother Jones." They were stopped by a line of troops on horseback. Reports differ on what happened next. Did the women try to rush through the line of soldiers—or was it a "militia riot"? A UMW organizer sent a telegram to headquarters in which he described the scene. "Woman carrying American flag knocked down with butt of gun and flag torn from her hands by

Mary leading a parade to publicize the plight of the miners in southern Colorado.

militiamen. Cavalrymen slashed another woman with a saber almost severing an ear from her head. Militiamen jab sabers and bayonets into backs of women. . . . Feeling is intense. Union officers doing everything to pacify people."

General Chase stated coolly that Mary was a "dangerous rabble-rouser" whom he would be pleased to release—if she would leave the area. "Most of the acts of violence committed in the strike region have been inspired by this woman's incendiary rhetoric," he said. Trinidad was rife with rumors that the miners were planning an all-out assault on the militia, and then word came that Congress had ordered an investigation of the Colorado strike to begin immediately.

On February 9, the federal commission began hearings in Denver. Soon after, Governor Ammons ordered over half the militia withdrawn from the strike zone. In the beginning of March, when the commission came to Trinidad, Mary was suddenly and unceremoniously released. She was taken to Denver, where, she was told, the governor wished to see her.

In the executive office in the capitol building the governor paced back and forth for several minutes before speaking. Then he talked about how dangerous the situation was. The strike zone, he said, was certainly no place for an old woman.

"I am going to turn you free," he said. "But you must not go back there."

"Governor," Mary replied, "I am going back."

"I think you ought to take my advice and do what I think you ought to do," the governor said.

Mary turned toward the door, then back again.

"Governor," she said, "if Washington took instructions from such as you, we would be under King George's descendants yet! If

Lincoln took instructions from you, Grant would never have gone to Gettysburg. I think I had better not take your orders."

A few days later, Mary left Denver for Trinidad once again. Before boarding the train, she wrote a letter to the Powderlys. "I leave again tonight for the field of battle," she said. "I suppose that just as soon as I get to Trinidad I will be arrested. . . . You can watch the [news]papers."

Mary boarded the train, but she never reached Trinidad. And even if the Powderlys hadn't been looking for news of her, they couldn't have missed it. For the next day, it made headlines in almost every major newspaper in the country.

General Chase halted the train at Walsenberg at five-thirty in the morning. Militiamen boarded, guarded the exits, and searched the compartments for Mary. She was taken off the train and placed in the cellar of the county courthouse. There was no hearing. She was not charged with any crime.

"It was cold," Mary wrote, "it was a horrible place, and they thought it would sicken me, but I concluded to stay in that cellar and fight them out. I had sewer rats that long every night to fight, and all I had was a beer bottle; I would get one rat and another would run across the cellar at me. I fought the rats inside and out just alike."

Days passed. It was hard for Mary to keep track of them. She had little to do but peer out the basement window at the feet of the people on the sidewalk above. There were "miners' feet in old shoes; soldiers' feet well clad in government leather; the shoes of women with the heels run down; the dilapidated shoes of children; barefooted boys. The children would scrooch down and wave to me but the soldiers shooed them off."

Telegrams flooded the governor's office and the White House.

General Francisco (Pancho) Villa offered a trade to President
Wilson. He would release a prisoner in a Mexican jail if Wilson
"would show the same regard for humanity toward one of your
own citizens, a woman past eighty years, who is being illegally
deprived of her liberty. . . . I refer to Mother Jones."

Soon after Villa's wire, Mary managed to have a letter, addressed to the American people, smuggled out of prison. It was
published in newspapers all around the country.

To My Friends and the Public Generally:
    I am being held a prisoner incommunicado in a damp
underground cell. . . . Have been here since 5:30 A.M. of the
23rd of March, when I was taken from the train by armed
soldiers, as I was passing through Walsenberg. I have discovered what appears to be an opportunity to smuggle a

Strikers' wives in Trinidad demonstrate on Mary's behalf.

letter out of prison and shall attempt to get this communication by the armed guards which day and night surround me . . .

I want to say to the public that I am an American citizen. . . . and I claim the right of an American citizen to go where I please so long as I do not violate the law . . . I ask the press to let the nation know of my treatment and to say to my friends . . . that not even my incarceration in a damp underground dungeon will make me give up the fight in which I am engaged for liberty and for the rights of the working people. To be shut from the sunlight is not pleasant but . . . I shall stand firm. To be in prison is no disgrace.

After twenty-six days, Mary was suddenly released. No charges were ever filed against her. No explanation was given. She was

weak from the ordeal but very glad to learn that the federal
Commission on Mines and Mining had resumed hearings, partly
as a result of the publicity caused by her arrest. She went directly
to Washington to speak before the commission.

John D. Rockefeller, Jr., had been called to testify the week
before. He had explained politely that he was opposed to unions
because they "dictated" to the workers and "deprived them of
their freedom." "I have been so greatly interested in the matter,"
the well-dressed, well-groomed gentleman said, "and have such a
warm sympathy for this very large number of men that work for
us, that I should be the last to surrender the liberty under which
they have been working and the conditions which to them have
been entirely satisfactory, to give up that liberty and accept
dictation from those outside who have no interest in them or in
the company."

One of the commissioners asked Rockefeller whether he was
"willing to let these killings take place rather than to go there and
do something to settle conditions."

Rockefeller answered that his interest in labor was "so
profound," and that he believed "so sincerely" in the "principle of
open camps" (that is, nonunion camps), that he would stand by his
officers "at any cost."

"And you will do that even if it costs all your property and kills
all your employees?"

"It is a great principle," Mr. Rockefeller replied.

The commission found his explanations difficult to believe.
"One must conclude," the report said, "that he would rather
spend the money of the company for guns, pay of detectives and
mine guards and starve the miners into submission."

When Mary spoke before the commission some days later, she

described what she had seen and the way she had been treated at the hands of the Colorado authorities. One of the investigators asked her whether she had "encouraged the disruptions of the peace," and he read some of the speeches Mary had given in West Virginia as examples. They seemed almost indefensible—especially when read by the dignified Congressman in the quiet, orderly chamber. But Mary defended herself by referring to another figure who had been caught up in violent passions and bitter struggles. "That is not half so radical as Lincoln," she replied calmly. "I have heard him make a great deal more radical speech."

Another Congressman asked Mary what crime she had been charged with when she was arrested by the militia. She explained that she had not been charged with any crime, but had simply been imprisoned. Then, urging the commission to take seriously the power which the militia wielded, she told them about the peaceful meetings that had been disrupted, the tent colonies which had been raided, the men who had been killed. The "open camps" Mr. Rockefeller favored would be fine, she said, if the government and not Mr. Rockefeller owned the mines. As it was, the workers were being "starved and robbed and plundered and shot."

Mary promised the commission that she would do everything in her power to stop the disorder and bloodshed, and she ended her testimony with a plea that President Wilson at least abolish the mine guard system—if he would not take over the mines entirely—and "get the gunmen out of the state."

Mary's testimony created a great deal of favorable publicity for the Colorado strikers. And it brought forth a furious attack from Representative George Kindel, a Congressman from Colorado who did not wish the government to investigate conditions in his state. In Congress the next day, Kindel attacked Mary, calling her a "notorious and troublesome woman" who, together with other "outside agitators," were keeping Colorado in turmoil. The miners were satisfied and peaceful until these people came in and started trouble. What right did Mary have to come to Colorado in the first place? he asked. What right did she have to interfere in other people's business, to mix in where she did not belong? What kind of a woman was she?

In answer to his question, Representative Kindel read the old account given of Mary in *Polly Pry* in 1904. He read the entire two articles aloud, so that they would be included in the *Congressional Record.* Now anyone who ever wished to learn about Mother Jones, he announced, would learn that she had been accused, in the halls of Congress, of being a prostitute.

The Powderlys, with whom Mary was staying, were very disturbed, although Mary herself was not. Terence wrote to Kindel, telling the Congressman that he personally had known Mary during part of the time when the "events" described were supposed to have taken place. He knew for a fact that they were not true. At the least, Powderly said, Kindel should ask that the articles be erased from the *Congressional Record.* He accused Kindel of having "assailed a white-haired, aged, defenseless woman."

Kindel did not respond to Powderly's letter.

On April 19, a Sunday, Mary was still in Washington. She spent the day in the country with the Powderlys. Everything was in bloom.

The nineteenth was a glorious day in Colorado too, the first day of real spring. In the tent colony at Ludlow, a celebration was going on. April 19 was the Greek Easter, and many of the miners there were Greek immigrants. People danced, they organized baseball games, and they sang. Dinner was a special feast of carefully prepared Greek dishes. For a time, even the machine guns which looked down on the colony from the hill beside it were almost forgotten. In the evening, there were bonfires and more songs. The children sang a new version of "The Battle Hymn of the Republic." Before they went to their tents to sleep, the entire colony joined in.

> *There's a fight in Colorado for to set the miners free,*
> *From the tyrants and the money-kings and all the*
> *   powers that be;*
> *They have trampled on the freedom that was meant*
> *   for you and me,*
> *But Right is marching on.*
>
> *Cheer, boys, cheer the cause of union,*
> *The Colorado Miners Union,*
> *Glory, glory to our Union,*
> *Our cause is marching on.*

Feelings were high and hopeful, but even so, watchmen took up their regular positions around the colony as the rest of the people went to bed.

The next morning, just after dawn, the watchmen ran through the colony. They yelled for everyone to dress quickly, and to be on the alert. Two companies of militia stationed on the neighboring hillside had begun to drill.

Then, three signal bombs burst in the sky over the soldiers' camp. The miners grabbed their weapons and ran to defend the colony.

"Suddenly," wrote journalist John Reed, "the machine guns pounded stab-stab-stab full on the tents. The most awful panic followed. Some of the women and children streamed out over the plain, to get away from the tent colony. They were shot at as they ran." One young boy was killed running to his tent to get his kitten. A group of people reached the well at the pump house and climbed down the inside on long ladders. Still others crept into the pits which had been dug underneath the tents as a safety measure.

"Explosive bullets," Reed wrote, "burst with the report of a six-shooter all through the tents." The miners who were armed stationed themselves around the colony, and tried to draw the soldiers' fire away from the tents themselves. But "the machine guns never let up." One of the commanders, Lieutenant Linderfelt, ordered his troops to "shoot every Goddamned thing that moves."

The strikers' tent colony at Ludlow.

At seven-thirty, soldiers set the first tent on fire. Soon other fires were set, and within minutes tents throughout the colony were ablaze.

The militiamen walked through the burning campsite, pulling the last people from their tents, beating and kicking them as they herded them together. Reed reported that one striker, a man named Snyder, was found in his tent crouching beside the body of his eleven-year-old son. A militiaman came inside, soaked the tent with kerosene and set it on fire. He hit Snyder with his rifle, and told him to "beat it." Snyder pointed to the body of his boy, "and the soldier dragged it outside by the collar, threw it on the ground, and said, 'Here! Carry the damned thing yourself!' "

The next morning, when the fires had died out and the troops were gone, those who survived returned. Where the tent colony had been was a square of "ghastly ruins." "Stoves, pots and pans still full of food . . . baby carriages, piles of half-burned clothes, children's toys, all riddled with bullets," was all that was left. Beneath the wreckage of one of the tent sites, in the pit in which they had been hiding, were the burned bodies of eleven children and two young mothers.

The massacre at Ludlow shocked and shamed the nation. It was a story of "horror unparalleled in the history of industrial warfare," wrote *The New York Times* beneath a headline which read, "Women and Children Roasted in Pits of Tent Colony as Flames Destroy It." Colorado exploded in open rebellion, as miners from the surrounding colonies and other citizens armed themselves and came to Trinidad. They took over the city, as well as towns, mines, and villages for 200 miles around Ludlow. They set fire to buildings that were owned by the CFI and battled against any state troops or company troops who dared to stop them. The sheriff and deputy sheriffs of Trinidad barricaded themselves in the basement of the county courthouse. For several days, a congressional report stated, "there was positive danger of a national revolution growing out of this Colorado strike." The state militia and the company guards were no longer in control.

Governor Ammons appealed to the federal government for troops with which to put down the "open insurrection against the state." And now, the federal government acted. Soldiers were ordered into Colorado on April 29. The state militia was withdrawn. The inflow of strikebreakers stopped. The fighting came to an end.

Mary returned from Washington at about the same time and addressed a crowd on the steps of the capitol building in Denver. The crowd "screamed its approval" when Mary appeared, "took off her bonnet and threw up a clenched fist in welcome."

"Here I am again, boys," Mary said, "just back from Washington and you aren't licked by a whole lot. Washington is aroused and there is help coming. We'll make some laws to put the Colorado Fuel and Iron Company out of business—and Mr. Rockefeller too."

Mary was referring to the federal committee which was on its way, under instructions from President Wilson, to work out a settlement of the strike that would be acceptable to both sides. She was confident that the end was in sight.

A month later, the committee presented its proposal. It suggested a three-year truce, binding on both the owners and the miners, and the rehiring of all miners who had not been convicted of crimes. It also recommended an eight-hour day and an increase in wages. It did not state that the union should be recognized as the representative of the workers, leaving that issue to be handled

The Ludlow colony after the fire.

by the parties themselves. This was a blow to the UMW, but its leaders felt they had no choice. They recommended that the miners vote to accept the proposal—and they did. Then the coal companies, in an act of stunning arrogance, turned it down.

At this, Mary returned to Washington for a meeting with President Wilson. She pleaded with him to take the mines away from the companies and turn them over to the federal government. "Coal is a mineral," she said. "No operator, no coal company on the face of the earth made it. It belongs to the nation. It was there down through the ages and it belongs to every generation that comes along." The UMW, in despair of ever reaching an agreement with the companies, later made the same request.

But President Wilson would not do that. Instead, he established a special commission to act as a court of appeals in the case of future disputes between the miners and the companies. Though he sympathized with the miners, he urged the union to accept the commission as a stopgap measure and to call an end to the strike. On December 7, 1914, the miners returned to work. They returned on the companies' terms, under conditions almost identical to those which had existed before the strike.

Rockefeller, Mary recalled, tried to counter the "bad publicity" the strike had created for his company. He bombarded the country with pamphlets showing "how perfectly happy was the life of the miner until the agitators came; how joyous he was with the . . . company's pigstys for homes, the company's teachers and preachers and coroners. How the miners hated the . . . eight-hour working day, begging to be allowed to work ten, twelve. . . . and all the while, the mothers of the children who died at Ludlow were mourning their dead."

Later in the year, Mary tried to explain the defeat to a crowd of thousands in New York City's Cooper Union. "The union lost in Colorado," she said bitterly, because "on their side the workers had only the Constitution. The other side had bayonets."

✂ FOURTEEN ✂

THE STEELWORKERS

Mary left Colorado in the winter of 1915, but she kept in touch with the people there, returning several times to visit, to bring money collected at meetings, to bring food and clothing. In the spring, when a federal commission began an investigation of the strike, Mary testified. After again describing the horrors she had seen, she repeated what she had said to President Wilson in private: company guards and detectives must be outlawed—and the federal government itself must take over the mines.

For the next year and a half, Mary traveled almost continuously. War had just broken out in Europe, and already there was talk of America's entry. Many of Mary's friends, including Haywood and Debs, opposed the war. They called it a "war of the capitalists" and thought that the powers were in it only to increase their own wealth. They believed working people should not fight the battles of the rich. Mary was inclined to agree, but she did not become involved in any of the demonstrations called to protest America's entry into World War I. Instead, she traveled from state to state, joining now one group of strikers, now another in a path that zigzagged across America. She was with striking garment workers in Chicago, factory workers in New Jersey, streetcar operators in New York. "I live in America," she said to one reporter. "But where I do not know. My address is like my shoes. It travels with me."

Though Mary rarely took part in electoral politics, she traveled to Indiana to help Senator John Kern when the 1916 elections came around. Kern was the man who had spoken up for the West Virginia strikers and who had read Mary's telegram from prison to the U.S. Senate. Mary traveled through the mining districts of Indiana, urging the people to send Senator Kern back to Washington. Kern lost the election, but he expressed his gratitude to Mary for her support before she returned to New York. Soon she was traveling again, this time to California to help a man named Tom Mooney. He was a socialist and a pacifist, and because he was strongly opposed to America's entry into World War I, he was considered a dangerous radical by many people in the government. Mooney had been arrested in the summer, when a bomb exploded at a Prepare-for-War parade in San Francisco. He was charged with the crime and taken to prison to await a trial. From there he wrote Mary an appeal for help.

"I will do everything I can," Mary wrote back, ending her letter, "I am yours in the struggle for a nobler civilization." Then she set out for California.

Many people were working for Mooney, and Mary joined the

effort, making speeches and collecting funds for his defense. But he had been branded a "traitor," and feelings against him were strong.

The trial began in January, on the eve of America's entry into the war. Mooney's opposition to it was enough to persuade many people that he was "lawless" and capable of any sort of crime. At the trial, a photograph was produced—with a clock in the background—which showed that Mooney and his wife were far from the scene at the time of the explosion. But he was found guilty, and in May, 1917, he was sentenced to death by hanging.

Throughout the summer and fall, Mary toured the West Coast, raising money and bringing the story to as many people as would listen. On Mooney's behalf, she even addressed the Women's Christian Temperance Union, an organization which was formed to fight against what it considered a dangerous social evil—the consumption of alcoholic beverages. In many states, legislatures had already passed "dry laws" which prohibited buying and selling whiskey and all other drinks containing alcohol. Mary thought the "temperance movement" was foolish, but the WCTU had a great deal of influence. She swallowed her criticism of its aims and appealed to them to join the struggle for Tom Mooney. She told them that in the minds of America's working people, the Mooney case was a test of the justice of American courts. Mooney must be cleared or the workers would lose faith in the system. If that happens, she said, "all hope is blasted and no one can be responsible for the outcome."

The publicity Tom Mooney's case received did not get him a new trial, but it saved him from the gallows. In April of 1918, just before he was to be hung, the governor of California gave him a reprieve and then changed the sentence from death to life imprisonment. Mooney remained in prison for twenty-two years before he was pardoned and freed.

Mary was still on the West Coast in the summer of 1918 when she learned that a National Committee had been formed to organize the workers in the steel industry. In other industries, workers had made some gains during the war, for it had created a general shortage of manpower at the same time that production intensified. In some cases, employers had even accepted their workers' right to have a union represent them. But in the steel industry, workers continued to labor twelve hours a day, six days a week. Twenty-five years earlier, millionaire Andrew Carnegie, president of the Carnegie Steel Corporation, and his general manager,

Mary in Monessen, Pennsylvania, with leaders of the 1919 strike. William Foster is to the right, just behind Mary.

Henry Frick, a millionaire in his own right, destroyed the fledgling Iron and Steelworkers Union in the brutal "Battle of Homestead." A dozen men had been killed, hundreds wounded, and 3,200 out of 4,000 workers blacklisted so that they could never work in the steel industry again. "We had to teach our employees a lesson and we have taught them one they will never forget," Frick had cabled to Carnegie, who was vacationing in Scotland. "Life worth living again," Carnegie cabled back. "Congratulations to all around."

Now union organizers, under the guidance of the American Federation of Labor, were preparing to try once again. Mary decided to go east to help.

William Z. Foster was one of the leaders of the National Committee, and it was to him that Mary went when she arrived in Pittsburgh. Foster explained that the steelworkers were difficult to organize because most of them were immigrants and spoke very little English. They had been hired for that very reason, he said, for immigrants were easier to control than native Americans, and would work for lower wages. In addition, the steel towns had been "closed" to union organizers. The companies had been able to persuade local judges to issue injunctions prohibiting meetings and speeches of any kind—even on street corners and empty lots. Committee organizers were working in spite of the injunctions, and as a result, at any given time, half of them were in jail.

Mary set out immediately. She traveled up and down the Monongahela River, speaking to thousands of workers in dozens of towns. Even when they could not understand what she was saying, they came to the meetings, and they stayed. "They would stand for hours," she wrote, "fitting the English words to the feelings in their hearts. Their patient faces looked up into mine."

Sometimes Mary stayed ahead of the sheriffs. Sometimes she did not.

In Monessen, just a little way from Pittsburgh, Mary led 10,000 workers in a parade to protest the injunctions which had closed the meeting halls to them.

In Sharon and Farrell, where "the lick-spittle authorities," as she called them, had forbidden all meetings, thousands of workers crossed the river and held a meeting in Ohio, "where the Constitution of the United States instead of the steel corporation's constitution was law."

But in Homestead, she was arrested. There, at the place where company guards had battled unionists twenty-five years earlier, Mary called U.S. Steel President Elbert Gary "Kaiser Gary," in a pointed comparison between him and the German monarch the United States had just defeated in the First World War. "We are going to see whether Pennsylvania belongs to Kaiser Gary or to Uncle Sam," she said. "If Gary's got it, we are going to take it away from him and give it back to Uncle Sam." The audience cheered. "Our Kaisers sit up and smoke seventy-five-cent cigars," Mary continued, "and have lackeys with knee pants bring them champagne while you starve, while you grow old at forty, stoking their furnaces."

Suddenly, Mary and the other two organizers were pulled from the speakers' platform by, in Mary's words, "the steel bosses' sheriffs." They were arrested and taken to the county jail. But the workers followed them there and milled around outside, demanding Mary's release. The sheriff panicked.

He asked Mary if she would speak to the crowd gathered in front of the jail. "I went outside and told the boys that they should go home now," she wrote. "I told them I would be released on bond soon, and that they should go home and wait for word."

The crowd was calmed, the men went home, and Mary was released on fifteen dollars' bond. Two days later, the case was brought to trial.

Mary knew that she had the United States Constitution on her side. Specifically, she had the First Amendment. It guaranteed "the right of the people peaceably to assemble." But money rather than the law made the rules that day. Mary described the scene in her *Autobiography*.

A "cranky judge," she wrote, had asked her if she had a permit to speak on the streets. When she replied that she did, the judge demanded to know who issued it.

"Patrick Henry," Mary replied, "Thomas Jefferson, and John Adams."

The "old steel judge" was not impressed and fined the organizers heavily.

In spite of the injunctions and arrests, by December, over 60,000 steelworkers had joined the union. By June, 1919, the figure reached 100,000. By September, although the National Committee wanted to continue the organizing drive, the workers were eager to take action. Samuel Gompers, president of the American Federation of Labor, wrote to President Gary of U.S. Steel. He told him how many men had joined the union, and he asked for a conference so they could discuss the situation. Gary ignored the request. The National Committee then contacted President Wilson and asked him for his help in persuading Gary to meet with them. President Wilson tried, but Gary refused.

Mary called Gary "a czar," and said that he had insulted the whole nation by refusing the President's request. But "what did it matter to him," she wrote, "that thousands upon thousands of men ... worked in front of scorching furnaces 12 long hours, through the day, through the night. ..." He met his workers "as is the customary way with tyrants. ... He ordered forth his two faithful generals: fear and starvation, one to clutch at the worker's throat and the other at his stomach and the stomachs of his little children."

At a meeting of workers' representatives, a vote was taken to determine whether or not to call a strike. The result: 98 percent voted to strike "if the companies continued to refuse to negotiate."

On September 22, the strike began. In spite of General Fear and General Hunger, almost 400,000 people walked off their jobs. Even the National Committee was surprised by the huge number, far greater than the number of workers who had actually signed their names to the union charter. "Kaiser Gary," who had claimed that the workers did not want the union and would never support a strike, was silent.

The members of the National Committee dug in their heels for a long struggle. The number of people involved made strike activities very difficult to plan and coordinate. And the strikers were spread out through fifty towns in ten states. Nevertheless, the strike was so enthusiastically supported that, in the first days, it seemed as though they might win—if not everything, at least the most important thing, their right to belong to a union and to have the union act as their official representative.

But soon it was clear that the companies had the upper hand. With the "steel judges" and "steel sheriffs" working for them, they drove the strikers underground. Injunctions made all meetings illegal—and any gathering of more than three or four people was considered a "meeting." Foster himself was not allowed to have chairs in his office, because chairs, the authorities said, indicated that he "planned" to hold a meeting. "Here men gathered in silent groups," Mary wrote, "in whispering groups, to get what word they could of the strike."

The organizers tried to keep the strikers informed by word of mouth. But the companies maneuvered cleverly to counter their attempts. They planted spies among the strikers and circulated false reports about the strike's progress. Some company agents, pointing to the "U.S." in the title of the major steel company, United States Steel, tried to convince the immigrants that the company was part of the government, and that the strike was actually a rebellion they should not take part in. In Pennsylvania, agents told the workers that the Ohio strike was collapsing. In Ohio, they said that it was over in Pennsylvania. With information so hard to come by, and even harder to keep track of, it was often impossible for the men to distinguish truth from rumor. "With meetings forbidden," Mary wrote, "with mails censored, with no means of communication allowed, the strikers could not know of the progress of their strike."

Soon the companies tried another tactic, designed to prevent the American people from helping or even sympathizing with the steelworkers. They claimed that the strike was not a true strike at all but was part of a plot, directed by foreign agents, to destroy the American economy and take over the United States. What foreign country was behind it? The Soviet Union, the story ran, the new country created in 1918 after the Russian people had revolted and overthrown their ruler, Czar Nicholas II. The leaders of the Soviet Union claimed that they had created a workers' republic and that soon the working people of Europe and the United States would join them and launch revolutions of their own. It was

A poster distributed by steel plant owners, implying that the government wants the strikers to return to work. "Go Back to Work" is written in eight languages.

widely believed that the Soviet Union was sending agents to other countries to help start revolutions. A wave of fear resulted, which came to be called "The Red Scare." Many people saw the hand of "foreign agents" and "revolutionaries" everywhere. Hundreds of people in the United States had already been arrested and charged with plotting to overthrow the government.

It was easy for the steel corporations to use this situation to their advantage. They said the strike was being controlled by Moscow and was sponsored and supported by Soviet agents. Newspapers, which Mary accused of having sold out to the companies, printed articles and stories claiming that the workers had no real problems—and no reason for calling a strike. Then

221

they described the foreign agents who were behind it.

The campaign worked. Public opinion was soon solidly against the steelworkers. "We could not get the story of the struggle of these slaves over to the public," Mary reported. "The press groveled at the feet of the steel gods. The local pulpits dared not speak. Intimidation stalked the churches, the schools, the theaters. The rule of steel was absolute."

Now the police, public and private, were given a free hand. The hated Pennsylvania Coal and Iron Police rode through the streets on horseback, beating strikers, arresting people at random. Strikebreakers were brought in, and several of the mills went back into operation. The guards "broke up the picket lines," Mary wrote, "but worse than that, they broke up the ideal in the hearts of thousands of foreigners . . . their dream that America was a government for the people—for the poor and the oppressed."

Visiting the strikers in their homes, Mary found entire families huddled indoors, too frightened to step outside. "The guards chase us out of our own yards, Mother," one young wife told her. "And the kids are frightened. The guards chase them into the house too. If the men walk out, they get chased by the mounted police. If they visit another house, the house gets raided and the men get arrested for 'holding a meeting.' They daren't even sit on the steps. Officers chase them in."

Foster praised Mary for her courage and endurance. "Mother Jones lent great assistance to the steelworkers," he said, "dauntlessly going to jail and meeting the hardships and dangers of the work in a manner that would do credit to one half her age." But in the press, she was portrayed as an unreasonable, wild-eyed revolutionary. Some of her speeches made the press's job easy. "So this is Gary," she said in a speech in late October. "Well, we're going to change the name and we're going to take over the steel works and we're going to run them for Uncle Sam. It's the damned gang of robbers and political thieves that will start the American revolution and it won't stop until every last one of them is gone." Then she said the words that made headlines and sold thousands of newspapers the next day. "I'll be ninety years old the first of May. But by God if I have to, I'll take ninety guns and shoot hell out of 'em!"

As fierce as Mary may have sounded, and as dangerous as the press made the strikers seem, in fact the strike had been crippled from the start and was now about to collapse. Hundreds had already been arrested. Hundreds more were injured in raids. And twenty-six people were killed—all of them steelworkers or unionists.

Mary continued to travel to the steel towns in the Pittsburgh area, but it had become impossible to hold meetings. In fact, unionists could hardly walk through town without drawing the fire of the police. "If I were to stop and talk to a woman on the street about her child," Mary wrote, "the cossacks would come charging down upon us, and we would have to run for our lives. If I were to talk to a man in the streets of Braddock, we would be arrested for unlawful assembly."

The National Committee again requested a conference with President Gary. But he replied that there were "no issues to discuss." The strikers began to return to the mills. By December, less than one quarter were still out. By January, 1920, Mary wrote, the strike had "shivered to pieces." The National Committee sent out an announcement. "All steelworkers are now at liberty to return to work."

At headquarters, Mary wrote, "men wept. I wept with them."

Mounted police officer threatening a union organizer during the steel strike.

It was over. And yet, as Mary watched the night sky, red from the glare of the furnaces, she felt, as she had always felt, that peace cannot be permanent unless it is accompanied by justice. People may be beaten and silenced for a time, but not forever. "Injustice boils in men's hearts," she wrote, "as does steel in its cauldron, ready to pour forth, white hot, in the fullness of time."

THE LAST YEARS

In the spring of 1920, with the steel strike behind her, Mary set out for California. She was suffering from rheumatism, as she had been off and on ever since the weeks she spent in "Rockefeller's prisons." The attacks always went as quickly as they came, and Mary was not one to fuss about her health. She didn't consider herself "ill" even now. But she was in pain, she admitted, and she was exhausted. When a friend, Katherine Schmidt, asked her to come to the West Coast to rest for a while, Mary was glad to go. It was a subdued Mother Jones who stepped off the train in Los Angeles. Mrs. Schmidt met her at the station and took her home. For the first time, Mary seemed old.

But the warm pleasant weather, and the quiet companionship of friends, soon had Mary up and about. In June she was giving interviews to reporters who were eager to hear her opinion on a very controversial issue: the Nineteenth Amendment to the Constitution, which had just been passed. For the first time, American women had the right to vote.

On the face of it, Mary should have been in favor of the amendment. The "suffrage movement," as the right-to-vote movement was called, included some of the most independent, outspoken women in the country. And wasn't the right to vote a basic right which should belong to every citizen? Surprisingly enough, Mary did not think so.

"In no sense of the word am I in favor of women's suffrage," she said. "Women already have a great responsibility on their shoulders. Home training of the child should be their task, and it is the most beautiful of tasks."

It was strange to hear this view from a woman who had lived a decidely "public" life, who had urged women to join their husbands on picket lines, who had unionized working women, who had in fact done her best to change an entire culture—and who had not had a home, or even a permanent address, for over fifty years. It was the traditional view of "woman's place," and it would not have been surprising from a woman who had lived a traditional life. But from the famous—and to some people infamous—Mother Jones, such a statement was astonishing.

Some of her friends may have wondered whether Mary was thinking of her own children when she spoke about motherhood. Perhaps the feeling of loss was sharp and painful still. Through the years, thousands of people had come to love Mary deeply, and thousands called her "Mother." But perhaps, as she neared the end of her life, she felt that she would have remained at home, a real mother to her own real children, if they had not been taken from her—and that ideally no woman should leave the home.

Mary disapproved of the suffrage movement on other grounds as well. It was not a "working-class movement," she said. Most of the women in it did not understand or care about the workers' struggle. The women's vote, if granted, would not make any difference to it. Sometimes Mary grouped the suffrage movement with the charity work and clubs in which "society women" had long been involved. These activities were not harmful in themselves, but they were not important either, according to Mary. They gave women of leisure something to do. "The plutocrats," Mary said once, referring to men of wealth and power, "have organized their women. They keep them busy with suffrage . . . charity and other fads."

To the women who had made real sacrifices for the movement, who had suffered abuse and criticism from many quarters in their fight for political equality, Mary's view was shocking and offensive. Taken in itself, it is puzzling. Even if the suffrage movement was not a working-class movement, the right to vote, if gained, would extend to working-class women. Wouldn't their votes be important? Although Mary had never been deeply involved in politics and was always a bit distrustful of the political arena, she knew that the vote could be an effective tool in the struggle for justice. She had campaigned for congressmen, presidents, and governors, believing that the right person in the right job could make a great deal of difference to the working class. Her observation that the suffrage movement was not a working-class movement may explain why she did not take part in it. But her conclusion that the women's vote would not help the workers does not seem logical. Nevertheless, she had criticized the movement on these grounds for years, and she did so now to the reporters who came to see her.

In the fall, Mary was traveling again, this time as the guest of the president of Mexico, Alvaro Obregon. He had invited her to come to Mexico City to attend a convention of the Pan American Federation of Labor.

Mary traveled with Fred Mooney (no relation to Tom Mooney). They had been friends since the days they had worked together in West Virginia. Mooney recalled that their train was stopped about forty miles outside Mexico City by a crowd of people who came rushing onto the tracks. At first Mary was alarmed. But then she and Mooney realized that the people were calling out a welcome.

"Madre Yones! Welcome to Mexico!" they yelled, throwing red carnations and blue violets into the air. Mary opened her window to wave at the people and soon the compartment was flooded with the beautiful flowers.

In Mexico City, Mary was given a car and a driver, and all her expenses were paid by the government. Wherever she went, she was greeted by cheering crowds. She was immensely pleased with the reception, and excited by the idea behind the Pan American Federation of bringing together all the working people in the hemisphere. "This is the beginning of a new day," she told a happy crowd at the convention, when "working people from all over the world will come together. . . . This is a great age," she said. "This is a great time to live in."

After the convention, Mary and Fred did some sightseeing. It was the closest thing to a real vacation Mary had ever had, and she was delighted. Mooney was concerned about her becoming

overtired, but she seemed to have as much energy as he did—
although she did turn down his invitation to climb with him to the
top of volcanic Popocatepetl! Sitting herself down, she laughed
and said that she had climbed her last mountain. But she urged
him to go ahead and try it.

Mary left Mexico, promising to return. A few months later, she
did, as the guest of General Villereal, one of the men she had
helped in 1908.

The Powderlys worried that a second trip might be too ex-
hausting. "I ask you always to bear in mind," Terence wrote,
"that there is only one Mother Jones. I doubt if the world has
seen her like before and, while I hope for the future, sadly feel the
world will not see her like again. Be careful then of your health
. . . guard it carefully and well."

Mary stayed in Mexico for two months. They were among the
most peaceful of her life. But Powderly's worries had been
realistic. Pleasant though the trip had been, Mary, ninety-two
years old, was exhausted by the time she returned to the United
States in the summer of 1922. Soon she was bedridden with a
severe attack of inflammatory rheumatism. Her hands were so
badly swollen that for several days she could not even hold a
spoon. The Powderlys took care of her. When they realized how
ill she was, they hired two private nurses to be with her around
the clock.

"Get-well" wishes arrived from labor assemblies, federations,
politicians, and private citizens all over the country. Friends
offered to take care of her if she was in any way a "burden" to the
Powderlys, but Terence and Emma would not hear of it. To a
friend who offered to help with the medical bills, Terence wrote:
"Now don't talk about paying me anything for what I do for

Mother Jones, that's a labor of love. My home is hers and as one of the family she don't count when it comes to expenses. Her fidelity to the labor movement is her claim with me and my wife feels the same way about it."

Reporters kept close tabs on Mary's condition. And soon— within the month in fact—the news was good. Mother Jones was up and feeling fine. A few weeks later, she was on the road again, on her way to Illinois.

Over the years, many people had asked Mary to write a book about her life, but other things had always seemed more urgent. Now, at the age of ninety-two, she decided to take on the task. An editor, Molly Field Parton, had volunteered to work with her on her autobiography, and as soon as Mary was well, she left to meet with Mrs. Parton in Chicago.

On the way, Mary stopped off in Springfield, Illinois, to visit with John Walker, a fellow organizer from the early days in West Virginia. The Powderlys had cautioned her to take things easy, but when Mary learned about a strike in a nearby town, she was concerned and wanted to help. "I am feeling better," she wrote to the Powderlys, "but I won't hold many meetings for I won't take any chances, but those poor shopmen have been out since last July and I feel if I am able to crawl I owe them a duty to give them a word of encouragement and let them know the sunshine of hope still throws out its rays."

By May, Mary was in Chicago working on her book. She found the writing tedious and slow. She was determined to see the project through to the end, but she doubted whether she would enjoy it. "I am getting so d—— tired writing this book," she wrote to Emma in June. "This work I am not used to." A few months later, Mary took time out from writing to address Chicago's striking dressmakers. It was a bitter strike, with blacklists, injunctions, and sweeping arrests. Mary urged the women to hold firm until "the bosses and their . . . lackeys" surrender. She didn't go on the picket lines this time, but she was glad to be out among the people again after spending so much time with pen and paper and words.

The book Mary and Molly Parton produced shows Mary's impatience and her lack of interest in details. The first thirty years of her life are dismissed in a few short paragraphs. Names are sometimes wrong and events are incorrectly dated. But Mary as a person comes through the pages. Her courage and her toughness are there, and her love for the people she tried to help, especially the miners.

Clarence Darrow agreed to write an introduction to Mary's book. He described her as "one of the most forceful" people in the American labor movement. "In all her career," Darrow said, "Mother Jones never quailed or ran away. Her deep convictions and fearless soul always drew her to seek the spot where the fight was hottest and the danger greatest. . . . In both the day and the night, in the poor villages and at the lonely cabin on the mountainside, Mother Jones always appeared in time of need."

During the year she spent in Chicago writing the book, Mary wrote often to the Powderlys. Terence became ill in the winter and in one of her letters to him, she scolded him lovingly for thinking too much about death, and she reminded him of the great things he had done. "You rocked the cradle of the movement," she had written to him earlier, "and made it possible for others to march on." Now she wrote, "Don't be thinking of the day you go away, think about the grand and glorious work you have done in the past and the work there is to be done in the future. Don't be dwelling on when we are going to take our final rest, we will have time enough to think of it."

In the spring, not a moment too soon as far as Mary was concerned, the book was finished and she headed back to Washington. But her reunion with the Powderlys was a sorrowful one. Terrence had never fully recovered his strength and in June, 1924, he died.

Over the next several years, Mary divided her time between Washington, where she stayed with Emma Powderly, and California, where she stayed with Mrs. Schmidt. She suffered more and more from rheumatism, and she found the warm sunny climate of the West Coast a great help. But wherever she was, letters came to her from "her boys." One miner cabled her:

Form 1204

CLASS OF SERVICE	SYMBOL
Day Message	
Day Letter	Blue
Night Message	Nite
Night Letter	N L

If none of these three symbols appears after the check (number of words) this is a day message. Otherwise its character is indicated by the symbol appearing after the check.

WESTERN UNION
TELEGRAM

NEWCOMB CARLTON, PRESIDENT

GEORGE W. E. ATKINS, VICE-PRESIDENT   BELVIDERE BROOKS, VICE-PRESIDENT

CLASS OF SERVICE	SYMBOL
Day Message	
Day Letter	Blue
Night Message	Nite
Night Letter	N L

If none of these three symbols appears after the check (number of words) this is a day message. Otherwise its character is indicated by the symbol appearing after the check.

RECEIVED AT   13 DS M 33 BLUE   5 ES

SHAMOKIN PA   1SEPT 11

VIA INDIANAPOLIS IND 12

MOTHER MARY JONES

CARE UNITED MINE WORKERS

ALBIA IA

MOTHER THERE IS A STRIKE AT THE SILK MILLS HERE WILL

YOU COME T ONCE I KNOW YOU CAN DO LOTS OF GOOD COME IF POSSIBLE

FROM A MINER

Telegram received at UMW headquarters.

In many speeches down through the years, Mary had described the dreams and wishes she had for others. But she never said very much about herself. Now she confided one to a friend. "Die when I may," Mary said, "I want it said of me by those who know me best, that I always plucked a thistle and planted a flower whenever I thought a flower would grow."

For the last year of her life, Mary was so ill that Emma Powderly could no longer care for her. A retired miner's family took her to their farm just outside of Washington. There she celebrated her hundredth birthday. Six months later, she died.

Mary Harris Jones lies buried where she had asked to be, in the Miners Cemetery in Mount Olive, Illinois. It was the only union-owned cemetery in America, purchased in 1898 when other cemeteries refused to bury four men killed by company detectives in a brutal strike at the nearby Virden mines. Mary had asked to be buried near the "Virden Martyrs," "to sleep under the clay with those brave boys."

A special train took her body from Washington to Illinois. Thousands of people, most of them miners, thronged the little town of Mount Olive and the Church of the Ascension. There were no relatives, and her coffin was carried by eight men, each representing a different union. A choir of miners sang the mass.

An honor guard stood at attention. They were miners too, most of them too young to have known Mary well. One had met her several years earlier when she came to visit his parents. "I knew she was a scrapper," the young miner said to a reporter, "and I expected to see a tough old person with a hard voice. Instead I saw an old-fashioned woman, kind of like the old ladies in the movies that sit at home and do embroidery. You couldn't have helped loving her."

Mary in her middle nineties. One of her last formal photographs.

So the story of Mary Jones came to an end. She had lived for one hundred years. Eugene Debs said she would be remembered by the children of the people she helped, "and their children's children forever." Mrs. J. Borden Harriman, wealthy member of the President's Commission on Industrial Relations, called her "the most significant woman in America." Governor George Hunt of Arizona said she was "unquestionably the greatest woman America has ever produced." And after her death, songs and poems were written about her by the people she had loved the most and tried the hardest to help, the miners. This one, whose author is unknown, was sung in the mountains of West Virginia.

> *The world today is mourning*
> *The death of Mother Jones*
> *Grief and sorrow hover*
> *Around the miners' homes.*
> *This grand old champion of labor*
> *Has gone to a better land,*
> *But the hard-working miners,*
> *They miss her guiding hand.*

The battles Mary waged were not won in her lifetime. She did not live to see the federal law, passed in 1933, which guaranteed the right of workers to form unions and required employers to meet with union representatives. She did not live to see the UMWA move openly and successfully into West Virginia and Colorado, protected by federal law. But perhaps the people who had known her remembered her deep strong voice crying out on the Charleston levee against the "mine-guard thugs," or her small lone figure being marched at gunpoint through the silent streets of Trinidad by soldiers with bayonets. She had been there when the struggle was bitter, and the people hopeless. She had helped them carry on.

Mary did not establish any institutions, start any movements, or found any new schools of thought. Her name does not appear on contracts, documents, or pieces of legislation. But she helped to change the lives of thousands of people. When they thought no one cared, she went to them. When they had no more hope, she inspired them. When the authorities commanded her to be silent, she challenged them to stop her if they could. She was effective whether in jail or out. For as long as she lived, she spoke to the nation about people who could not speak for themselves.

A few years after Mary's death, the sculptor Jo Davidson made a statue of her. It was placed in the lobby of the Department of Labor in Washington as a tribute to her memory. It is gone now, and today there are no public monuments in Mary's honor. She has taken her place in history beside the early union organizers she most respected. Their names have been all but forgotten, but the world is better because of their courage and devotion. "Their monuments are the good they did," Mary wrote of them, and the same may be written of her. Her monuments are not made of stone, but they are real and lasting—the hope she gave to others, the courage she inspired by her own example, and the dream of justice she left to all of us.

ఆ BIBLIOGRAPHY ఠ

BOOKS

Adam, G. Mercer. *Toronto, Old and New.* Ontario: Coles Publishing Co., 1974.

Adams, William F. *Ireland and Irish Emigration to the New World: 1815 to the Famine.* New Haven: Yale University Press, 1932

Addams, Jane. *Twenty Years at Hull House.* New York: Macmillan, 1966.

Brecher, Jeremy. *Strike!* San Francisco: Straight Arrow Press, 1972.

Brooks, Thomas R. *Toil and Trouble: A History of American Labor.* New York: Dell, 1972.

Capers, Gerald. *Biography of a River Town: Memphis, Its Heroic Age.* Chapel Hill: University of North Carolina Press, 1939.

238

Cromie, Richard. *The Great Chicago Fire.* New York: McGraw-Hill, 1958.

Dulles, Foster Rhea. *Labor in America.* New York: T. Y. Crowell, 1960.

Fetherling, Dale. *Mother Jones: The Miner's Angel, A Portrait.* Carbondale: Southern Illinois University Press, 1974.

Jameson, Anna. *Winter Studies and Summer Rambles in Canada.* Ontario: Coles Publishing Co., 1962 (originally pub. 1838).

Jones, Mary. *Autobiography of Mother Jones.* New York: Arno, 1969.

Long, Patricia. *Mother Jones, Woman Organizer.* Cambridge: The Red Sun Press Collective, 1976.

McIlwaine, Shields. *Memphis Down in Dixie.* New York: E. P. Dutton, 1948.

Mayer, Harold, and Wade, R. C. *Chicago: Growth of a Metropolis.* Chicago: University of Chicago Press, 1969.

Meltzer, Milton. *Bread and Roses, the Struggle of American Labor 1865-1915.* New York: Alfred A. Knopf, 1967.

Ray, Ginger. *The Bending Cross, A Biography of Eugene Debs.* New Brunswick: Rutgers University Press, 1949.

Spargo, John. *The Bitter Cry of the Children.* New York: Macmillan, 1968.

Ware, Norman. *The Industrial Worker: 1840–1860.* New York: Russell and Russell, 1968.

PERIODICALS

Acton, Janice, et al. "Schoolmarms and Early Teaching in Ontario." *Women At Work: Ontario, 1850–1930.* Ontario: Canadian Women's Educational Press, 1974.

Green, Archie. "The Death of Mother Jones." *Labor History* (Winter, 1960).

"Indomitable Spirit of Mother Jones." *Current Opinion* (July, 1913).

Jones, Mary. "A Picture of American Freedom in West Virginia." *International Socialist Review* (September, 1902).

———. "Civilization in Southern Mills." *International Socialist Review* (March, 1901).

Michelson, P. "Mother Jones." *Delineator* (May, 1915).

Ontario Department of Education. Annual Reports of the Normal, Model and Common Schools in Upper Canada for the Years 1845–6, 1847, 1849, and 1858.

UNPUBLISHED MANUSCRIPTS

Collier, Helen Camp. "Mother Jones and the Children's Crusade." Master's thesis, Columbia University, 1970.

Mikeal, Judith Elaine. "Mother Mary Jones: The Labor Movement's Impious Joan of Arc." Master's thesis, University of North Carolina, 1965.

❧ INDEX ❧